Benson

D1516591

Lessons from Nothing

CAMBRIDGE HANDBOOKS FOR LANGUAGE TEACHERS

This is a series of practical guides for teachers of English and other languages. Illustrative examples are usually drawn from the field of English as a foreign or second language, but the ideas and techniques described can equally well be used in the teaching of any language.

In this series:

Drama Techniques in Language Learning – A resource book of communication activities for language teachers
by Alan Maley and Alan Duff

Games for Language Learning
by Andrew Wright, David Betteridge and Michael Buckby

Discussions that Work – Task-centred fluency practice *by Penny Ur*

Once Upon a Time – Using stories in the language classroom
by John Morgan and Mario Rinvolucri

Teaching Listening Comprehension *by Penny Ur*

Keep Talking – Communicative fluency activities for language teaching
by Friederike Klippel

Working with Words – A guide to teaching and learning vocabulary
by Ruth Gairns and Stuart Redman

Learner English – A teacher's guide to interference and other problems
edited by Michael Swan and Bernard Smith

Testing Spoken Language – A handbook of oral testing techniques
by Nic Underhill

Literature in the Language Classroom – A resource book of ideas and activities *by Joanne Collie and Stephen Slater*

Dictation – New methods, new possibilities
by Paul Davis and Mario Rinvolucri

Grammar Practice Activities – A practical guide for teachers
by Penny Ur

Testing for Language Teachers *by Arthur Hughes*

The Inward Ear – Poetry in the language classroom
by Alan Maley and Alan Duff

Pictures for Language Learning *by Andrew Wright*

Five-Minute Activities – A resource book of short activities
by Penny Ur and Andrew Wright

The Standby Book – Activities for the language classroom
edited by Seth Lindstromberg

Lessons from Nothing – Activities for language teaching with limited time and resources
by Bruce Marsland

Lessons from Nothing

Activities for language teaching with limited time and resources

Bruce Marsland

CAMBRIDGE
UNIVERSITY PRESS

PUBLISHED BY THE PRESS SYNDICATE OF THE UNIVERSITY OF CAMBRIDGE
The Pitt Building, Trumpington Street, Cambridge, United Kingdom

CAMBRIDGE UNIVERSITY PRESS
The Edinburgh Building, Cambridge CB2 2RU, UK http://www.cup.cam.ac.uk
40 West 20th Street, New York, NY 10011–4211, USA http://www.cup.org
10 Stamford Road, Oakleigh, Melbourne 3166, Australia

© Cambridge University Press 1998

This book is in copyright. Subject to statutory exception
and to the provisions of relevant collective licensing agreements,
no reproduction of any part may take place without
the written permission of Cambridge University Press.

First published 1998
Reprinted 1999

Printed in the United Kingdom at the University Press, Cambridge

Typeset in Sabon 10½/12pt [CE]

A catalogue record for this book is available from the British Library

Library of Congress Cataloguing in Publication data
Marsland, Bruce.
Lessons from nothing: activities for language teaching with limited time and resources / Bruce Marsland.
p. cm. – (Cambridge handbooks for language teachers)
Includes bibliographical references (p.) and index.
ISBN (invalid) 0 521 62765 63 (pbk.)
1. English language – Study and teaching – Foreign speakers – Aids and devices. 2. English language – Problems, exercises, etc.
I. Title. II. Series.
PE1128.A2M343 1998
428′.007–dc21 98-24907
CIP

ISBN 0 521 62765 6 paperback

To my parents

Contents

Acknowledgements

Many thanks must go to the teachers and students who worked with me in Bulgaria, and whose ideas and enthusiasm were invaluable in collecting and trialling many of the activities contained in this book. Thanks too, for help and support, to: David Marsh (University of Jyväskylä), Sarah Donno, Lesley Gourlay, and of course Penny Ur and all at Cambridge University Press.

The author and publishers are grateful to the authors, publishers and others who have given permission for the use of copyright material identified in the text. It has not been possible to identify the sources of all the material used and in such cases the publishers would welcome information from copyright owners.

The Wylie Agency for the adapted extract on p. 55 from *The Man Who Mistook His Wife For A Hat* by Oliver Sacks © Oliver Sacks. All rights reserved; Janet Turnbull Irving and Bloomsbury for the adapted extract on p. 60 which is taken from the short story 'Almost in Iowa' in the book *Trying To Save Piggy Sneed* by John Irving published by Bloomsbury Publishing Plc in 1993; Faber and Faber Ltd for the extract on p. 66 from *Rosencrantz and Guildenstern are Dead* by Tom Stoppard; 'A Cat, A Horse and the Sun' on p. 68 from *Strictly Private* is reprinted by permission of The Peters Fraser and Dunlop Group Limited on behalf of Roger McGough © Roger McGough, 1981; the extract on p. 69 from *Under Milk Wood* by Dylan Thomas published by Everyman in 1985 is reprinted by permission of David Higham Associates and by permission of New Directions Pub. Corp.

Introduction

What is this book about?

This is a sourcebook of ELT exercises and activities which do not require extensive resources or facilities. It is primarily for teachers working in the developing world, although the materials are equally suitable for many other environments.

There are activities for all levels of proficiency, from beginner to advanced; and for all age groups, from young learners to adults. The emphasis is on providing practical ideas for teachers with limited access to resources – whether they are native speakers of English or not.

This book should also be useful for teachers who are working under the pressure of time, as many of the activities require little or no preparation. Young or trainee teachers should find assistance in this book, with the inclusion of several well established activities which can provide an excellent starting point for developing classroom technique, while more experienced teachers will find other relatively unknown activities, which might provide new ideas and inspiration.

Why is this book necessary?

Many excellent resource books have been written for EFL teachers, but most of them include a lot of activities which rely on certain facilities being readily available. Teachers in developing countries probably won't have access to video machines, OHPs or cassette recorders. The nearest photocopier could be many miles away. In some countries, teachers might not have a blackboard or even a classroom. Their students may not have pens or paper. And teachers in any environment can be pressed for time.

This collection of ideas is for teachers in situations like these.

What resources are required by this book?

About half the activities use, or can be adapted to use, no resources at all. They just require the teacher and students to be grouped together in one area.

Other activities are marked 'blackboard only'. This should really be 'chalk only', because often a blackboard can be improvised from wood, hardboard or other materials.

Some activities are marked 'pens/paper only', if you or your students require something to write on and with. A handful are activities which utilise blackboard, pens and paper.

The final section contains activities based on simple materials which can be supplied by you or your students from your homes.

None of the activities require the use of any electronic equipment.

What does a teacher need?

The most important requirements for using this book are enthusiasm, a good grasp of the English language, and a willingness to work hard and improvise. Some useful extra materials which could prove handy if you can get them would be:

- a selection of picture postcards or pictures from magazines
- packets of white and coloured chalk
- some paper and pens
- a packet of sticky address labels
- a book of poetry and/or short texts
- a good grammar reference book
- this and other teachers' handbooks and coursebooks

There are suggestions for the use of many of these things in this book.

Teachers in situations with limited time and facilities often rely on resource books of activities. Recommendations for books of texts, a grammar book, and teachers' handbooks of particular relevance appear in the annotated bibliography at the end of the book.

What are the methodological objectives of this book?

In a limited-resource situation, it can be very tempting to fall back on teacher-centred 'chalk and talk' lessons, and if there is no blackboard this can be reduced to plain 'talk'. Even without a textbook or other materials for support, it is possible for such an approach to have practical advantages for presenting new language structures.

In such circumstances, however, there is the danger of lessons having a lack of variety, leading to a loss of concentration and motivation for students, and even for the teacher. It is also easy for a teacher, whether experienced or not, to miss the warning signs until it is too late.

The aim of the language activities described in this book, therefore, is to focus students' minds onto the target language in varied and motivating ways, which encourage student-centred language discovery and self-development.

Without readily available books or photocopies, this will usually mean activities which are not based on extensive texts – although it does allow for the possibility of the teacher providing a newspaper, dictating an interesting text to the class, or copying a text onto a blackboard. The emphasis, though, will be on oral exercises and activities, and this in itself provides some advantages.

The necessity for communicative speech is one such advantage. With no written text to rely on, students need to make the effort to understand, and be understood by, the teacher. This leads to spoken interaction which can be more authentic and more 'human' than concentrating on books or cassettes. Simply using the target language when providing oral instructions for tasks and exercises gives the opportunity for a wide range of language as input, even without 'formal' listening work.

In turn, the authentic interaction which this entails means that the teacher–student relationship can be developed beyond the idea of 'demonstration' towards a feeling of 'co-operation'.

Hopefully teachers will be able to bear this in mind, and adapt and extend the ideas in this book for the requirements of their own unique situations. You might even be able to have some fun along the way!

How is this book organised?

The book is organised according to the resources needed for each activity. The first, and largest, section requires no resources at all. The number of resources required increases gradually through the book. Within the sections, the activities are ordered alphabetically.

Each activity is then clearly labelled to show the language-teaching point, language level, and recommended student age. The timing of each activity depends largely upon the size and ability of the class being taught. Occasional recommendations are given, but mostly the length of each activity is left to the discretion of the teacher.

How should the class be organised?

The activities here can be used in virtually any classroom, regardless of the physical limitations. They can be used outdoors if necessary. Several activities, however, are particularly, although not exclusively, suited to a circle of students. In large classes several such circles might be used, and in fixed classroom situations it is worth remembering that, as long as there is a fairly obvious sequence of participants, a 'circle' may be any shape – including a straight line!

Most of these 'circle' activities can be done either standing or sitting. Standing increases the energy of the activities, although for 'Change chairs' (5.1) sitting is an integral part of the exercise. It is also better for the atmosphere, and for giving examples, if the teacher includes himself or herself as part of the 'circle'. Also remember that the sequence of students answering questions does not always have to go the same way. For variation it can change direction on the word of the teacher, or a student can choose the next person to speak by naming or pointing at them. This is particularly useful in classrooms with fixed furniture, where a real circle is impossible.

Often, a lack of resources leads to very large class sizes. If your class is particularly large, some of the activities might need more adaptation, but most of the activities can be changed in this way, and several variations are given which take large classes into account.

What other types of activity are there?

Some activities have a competitive element. This can be utilised for individual or group rivalry, according to the nature of the class. Points, and even prizes, can be awarded if this helps motivation. Prizes don't have to be extravagant. Some children's classes might like having a special 'enjoyable' duty assigned to the winner. It is up to the teacher to judge the nature of each group, and to work with the resources available.

Other activities require collaboration rather than competition. On these occasions the class works together to find a solution to problems, or to complete a piece of work. Occasionally the teacher may have to prompt the less confident students, but it is worth remembering that many students learn from observation as well as from direct vocal involvement.

For many students, the most important part of the learning process is not the very active type of exercise traditional in TEFL, but is the time they have to themselves to contemplate and assimilate the language. There are also activities in this book which centre on individual students, and give them time for individual thought and discovery.

In addition, this book contains several activities which use drama in the classroom.

Why use drama?

One advantage of these drama exercises is that they can introduce situations which require a greater usage of English than is normally required in a simple 'classroom' scenario. Similarly, although not all drama activities require the use of character, extra 'people' can be brought into the class, which is a particular advantage when teaching small groups.

Many drama activities can be a very liberating experience, allowing experimentation with language in a more relaxed setting than the rigid class structure of grammar lessons. For this reason, it must be stressed that during such lessons, the teacher should not continually interrupt to correct mistakes in English. It is possible for the teacher to 'prompt' and provide 'models' without explicitly controlling the language output. Discretion should be the watchword. Any glaring mistakes can be noted for correction in later classes.

It is worth noting here, too, that as all the activities included in this collection, and the drama activities in particular, are intended to be student-centred rather than teacher-centred, it is the students – and not the teacher – who should be given the opportunity to practise their language. The sensitive teacher will realise this, and hopefully the activities in this book can consequently be more productive.

So, although the title of this book is *Lessons from Nothing*, by exploiting some of the ideas, teachers should be able to get beyond the notion that there is 'nothing to work with'. Instead, we will see that the possibilities for using language, imagination and human interaction change 'nothing' into a potentially limitless 'something'.

1 Activities using no resources

1.1 Action mimes

Language Continuous tenses

Level Elementary upwards

Age Young adult

This is a popular drama warm-up exercise which is usually done in a circle, but which can be easily used in any situation where students have at least some space in which they can stand up. It is especially useful for the initial presentation of tense forms, and for subsequent revision and comparison.

Procedure

1. Establish a set sequence in which students take their turn – along rows or around a circle, for example. If concentrating on the present continuous tense, the teacher begins with a target sentence like:

   'He is playing tennis.'

2. The next student in the series then mimes playing tennis, and thinks of another sentence:

   'She is typing a letter.'

3. This then passes on to the next student to mime, and so on. Encourage correct usage of 'he' and 'she'.

Variations

i) The mime is done first, and the next person guesses what the mime represents. This is particularly useful for demonstrating the use of other, awkward, continuous tenses, such as:

   'He was riding a bicycle.'
   'She has been behaving like a monkey.'

ii) Instead of using 'he' and 'she', use real names to indicate who should perform the action, therefore breaking the usual set sequence. This keeps everyone on their toes, and is a good 'getting-to-know-you' exercise with a new class.

1.2 Adverb game

Language Adverbs

Level Elementary

Age Any

Procedure

1. One student leaves the classroom, or moves out of earshot. The rest of the class decides on an adverb of action. When the class has thought of a suitable adverb, bring the first student back. He or she must now discover what the chosen adverb is by asking other students to perform actions in the manner of that adverb.
2. It will probably be impossible for the student to guess the adverb first time, so he or she continues by asking a different student to perform a different action using the same adverb. This carries on until the adverb is guessed correctly, or until the teacher decides that this will not happen (possibly after six or seven attempts). Another student then leaves the room, and the class decides on a new adverb.

This is a well tried and tested exercise, but it still produces some memorable and original sentences for students:

> 'Please blow your nose.' (Answer: romantically)
> 'Please stroke the cat.' (Answer: violently)

Preparation

If you are doing this exercise with a class for the first time, it might be worth having a small 'stock' of adverbs and commands ready to give them, which will then start them thinking of their own ideas. Possible examples at this early stage follow:

Examples of adverbs:

angrily, badly, carefully, carelessly, crazily, dangerously, happily, lazily, painfully, quickly, quietly, sadly, slowly, stupidly, violently.

Examples of commands:

do your homework, eat breakfast, feed the dog, get dressed, go for a walk, hitch a lift, play the violin, read a book, smoke a cigarette, take a shower, wait for a bus, watch TV.

Variation for large classes

An alternative method of presenting the exercise if you have a large class is to arrange students into sets of competing groups, which must then compile lists of adverbs for the other teams to guess. When the lists are ready, go to the first team, and allow any member of any other group to select an action for a member of that team to perform. The first person to guess the adverb being demonstrated wins a point for his or her team. Move on to the next group.

Alternatively, you may wish to have every member of the selected group performing the adverb, which removes the pressure from any one individual in that team.

1.3 Alibi

Language Question and answer forms; past tenses

Level Intermediate–Advanced

Age Adult upwards

This parlour game will be familiar to many teachers in some form. A crime (usually a hideous murder) is said to have been committed the previous evening. Build the tension by suggesting that three students in the class are suspected. Choose the students and name them.

Procedure

1. Ask these three students to leave the classroom (or move out of earshot) and devise their 'alibis' for the previous evening. Stress to them that they must know the *exact* details of what they did and

where they went. Also stress that they must claim to have been together the whole time.

2. While the three students are deciding on their story, split the rest of the class into three groups, each of which will interview each suspect in turn. If they have a pen and piece of paper, they can nominate a note-taker; otherwise the whole group will, like good detectives, have to rely on memory. Together, group members decide on some good questions to ask. They can also decide who will ask the questions, and where the suspect will sit (or stand).
3. After 5–10 minutes, bring the three suspects back into the classroom. One goes to each group for questioning, which can last for about five minutes, and then the groups swap suspects. All three groups get the chance to question all three suspects separately.
4. Any difference between the suspects' stories will be seen as proof of guilt. Maybe not all the suspects are guilty – it is up to the interrogating groups to decide. At the end of the questioning sessions, gather the evidence from the three groups orally, and take a class vote to decide which (if any) of the students is guilty.
5. If you have any time remaining, the class may wish to decide on a suitable punishment.

Acknowledgement

This method of setting up the activity comes from Penny Ur's book *Discussions That Work*.

1.4 Change it

Language Any

Level Elementary upwards

Age Any

Procedure

This is a substitution drill, which can be an effective method of getting students to focus on and internalise particular constructions, examples of which are given below. Such drills can be done in a circle if desired.

1. Begin with a single sentence, using the target language pattern:

   'The newspaper said the situation was unstable.'

2. In turn, students change any word in the sentence, and say the new sentence aloud. Anything which is both grammatical and comprehensible is permitted.

   'The newspaper said the mountain was unstable.'
   'The scientist said the mountain was unstable.'
   'The scientist thought the mountain was unstable.', etc.

Variations

i) If you wish to concentrate on adjective prefixes, for example, feed in a positive adjective, such as 'moral'. The next student repeats the initial sentence, but using the opposite of that adjective:

   'The newspaper said the situation was immoral.'

   Students change other words in the sentence to fit the new adjective:

   'The judge said the criminal was immoral.'

ii) If revising vocabulary sets such as 'food', start with:

   'Alan will take an apple on the picnic.'

   Give another name, for example Brian, and the next student must repeat the whole sentence using a food which begins with the same letter as the new name:

   'Brian will take a banana on the picnic.'

> *Possible language practice topics:*
>
> Comparatives; irregular verbs; opposites; prepositions of place (*in the box*, *on the wall*, etc.); pronouns; tenses and time phrases (*last week*, *tomorrow*, etc.); vocabulary sets.

Rationale

Drills like these can be very good if used occasionally for revision purposes, but should probably not be relied on too heavily as this could lead to demotivation.

1.5 Changes

Language Describing objects

Level Elementary upwards

Age Any

The purpose of this exercise is to describe how you might change the function of a place or object.

Procedure

If you are in a classroom, you could ask the class how they would change it into a prison cell, a doctor's surgery, a library, etc. If you have no classroom, you could choose any prominent local feature and ask students how to change it into an airport, a hospital, a zoo, or just into a better school.

> *Example:* Changing the park into a zoo (Intermediate level)
>
> 'Monkeys could live in those small trees.'
> 'We would have to build a cage to stop birds escaping.'
> 'There isn't enough water for crocodiles.'
> 'The lions would scare the horses if they were too close.'

Variation

If you have a blackboard available, ask students to draw their planned changes on it, labelling the additions and explaining how and why those changes should be made.

Variation for advanced students

Suggestions for changes are limited only by the imagination. With an advanced class you might even want to move on to describe changes which would make systems and processes more efficient: booking an appointment with a doctor; taking a book out of the library; taking money out of the bank, for example. You will probably find, however, that such changes are much more difficult to imagine and describe than the physical ones.

1.6 Cheating story

Language Narrative forms

Level Intermediate–Advanced

Age Any

This is really a variation of 'Guess the story' (1.18). However, in this case the teacher starts with no particular story in mind – although the class does not know that.

Procedure

1. The class is allowed twelve yes/no questions in an attempt to discover what they think the teacher's story is. The teacher answers 'no' to every third question, and 'yes' to all the others. Remember not to answer a question at all unless it is in good English. It is important throughout this exercise for the class to believe that they are 'discovering' the teacher's story, otherwise 'writer's block' might set in and obstruct the creative process. Therefore it is an idea to give the impression of careful thought before answering a question.
2. After asking twelve correctly formed questions, the class has to construct a story from the answers which they have been given. At this stage the teacher should not interfere by correcting the language. This can be done after the story has been completed.
3. After the exercise, you may wish to explain to the class how it was done. If you do this, remember that the next time you do the exercise you must use different rules to decide when to answer 'yes' or 'no'. Your students might even want to guess what these criteria are while they are asking questions.

Alternative rules:

'No' if a word in the question is repeated; 'Yes' otherwise.
'Yes' if a question uses the verbs 'do' or 'have'; 'No' for 'be' or modals.
'No' if a student hesitates when asking the question; 'Yes' otherwise.

Acknowledgement

This is adapted from an idea in Keith Johnstone's book *Impro*, in which he suggests answering 'yes' to any question ending in a vowel, 'maybe' to any question ending in the letter 'y', and 'no' to all other questions.

There are many other suggestions in his book which are relevant to the EFL classroom.

1.7 Clapping association

Language All vocabulary

Level Elementary upwards

Age Any

The first of this series of 'clapping' activities concentrates students' attention on word meanings through the use of a word association exercise.

Procedure

1. In the class, which could follow the 'circle' principles described in the introduction, set up a regular four-beat rhythm: clap hands twice, then click fingers twice. Students only speak during 'clicking' time, so 'clapping' time is their opportunity to think. Even though there are only two 'clicks', contributions need not be of two syllables. Words of up to four syllables can be used quite easily, as long as they can be fitted into the (approximately) two seconds allowed for each turn:

   <think> 'duck' <think> 'animal' . . . etc.
   [clap] [clap] [click] [click] [clap] [clap] [click] [click] . . .

2. Setting up the four-beat rhythm as a word-association drill means that each student must, in turn, shout out the first word he or she thinks of which is in any way associated with the previous word in the sequence. For example, if the teacher begins with the word 'duck', the sequence might continue:

   'water'–'blue'–'red'–'light'–'dark'–'night'–'sleep'–'dream'–etc.
   {('knight')–'king'–'queen'–etc.}

3. Any student (or the teacher) can stop the rhythm at any time to challenge an association. A reasonable explanation of the link between the two words in the sequence must then be given – in good English, of course – before the activity continues.

Rationale

The value of the exercise lies in helping students to think about the range of meanings underlying the words which they use. As this is an oral exercise, if an association is given which takes advantage of homophones (words which sound the same – such as 'night' being heard as 'knight' in the example above), then this is perfectly acceptable.

1.8 Clapping story

Language Narrative forms

Level Intermediate–Advanced

Age Any

This variation of the clapping activity allows students to produce their own original fictional material, which can then be utilised to revise past tense narrative forms.

Procedure

1. Within the four-beat rhythm, the teacher starts the first sentence of a story on the two clicked beats. A good way to start is 'There was', which introduces the past tense narrative form immediately, but leaves the topic and characters of the story to be decided by the class.
2. In turn, on the clicked beats, each student then adds two or three words to the story. The teacher stays in the 'circle' and can use this presence to keep the story going. Phrases such as 'but then', 'after that', 'so he', and 'however' are good for this purpose.
3. When you have a long enough story, stop the clapping and get students to try to remember as much of it as possible, and correct it into good English. The time lapse between the creation and the correction will have allowed them to identify some of their own mistakes, either automatically or by listening to others.
4. As a follow-up, students can be asked to act out portions of the story. Some of the material produced might allow the use of the 'Tableaux' activity (1.26) for more detailed language study.

1.9 Clapping verbs

Language Irregular verbs

Level Elementary upwards

Age Any

Procedure

1. Set up the four-beat rhythm as described above, but the teacher should be ready to speak on every third turn, using the list of irregular verbs below.
2. The teacher starts by calling out the infinitive of a verb. In time with the rhythm, the first student in the sequence calls out the past simple form, and the second calls out the perfect form. Then the teacher calls out another infinitive. The pattern continues around the 'circle'.
3. Encourage students to identify mistakes. Younger groups might like the idea of paying a forfeit for missing a turn or getting a word wrong. If your class is arranged in a real circle, running once around the circle might be a good energy-raising possibility. Otherwise some other suitable physical exercise (such as five press-ups) could be used, but it would probably be better to keep the verb sequence going while such forfeits are paid.

Rationale

This is an excellent way of revising irregular verb forms so that they become an automatic part of students' language. Don't be afraid to repeat the same verb during a session – it can only help students to memorise the forms.

Verbs for use with this exercise:

hit	(hit, hit)	leave	(left, left)	bite	(bit, bitten)
spend	(spent, spent)	fly	(flew, flown)	wake	(woke, woken)
beat	(beat, beaten)	meet	(met, met)	sell	(sold, sold)
swim	(swam, swum)	lay	(laid, laid)	wear	(wore, worn)
choose	(chose, chosen)	blow	(blew, blown)	hold	(held, held)
hide	(hid, hidden)	tear	(tore, torn)	hang	(hung, hung)
eat	(ate, eaten)	lie	(lay, lain)	shake	(shook, shaken)
throw	(threw, thrown)	rise	(rose, risen)	freeze	(froze, frozen)
teach	(taught, taught)	dig	(dug, dug)	catch	(caught, caught)
stick	(stuck, stuck)	fall	(fell, fallen)	feel	(felt, felt)
mean	(meant, meant)	sing	(sang, sung)	forget	(forgot, forgotten)

Variation for advanced students

For advanced groups, add other verbs to this list. You can even include regular verbs so that students have to remember if the form is '-ed' or not. But be sure to prepare your list in advance so that you can keep up with the pace of the exercise.

1.10 Clapping vocab

Language Vocabulary sets

Level Elementary upwards

Age Any

Procedure

1. Set up the four-beat rhythm as above. The teacher begins by calling out the title of the vocabulary set to be covered, for example, 'Animals'.
2. In time with the rhythm, the first student calls out the first animal he or she thinks of – for example, 'elephant'. This continues in the set sequence around the 'circle'. Repetitions are not allowed.

> *Possible vocabulary sets:*
>
> Animals; clothes; colours; countries; drinks; emotions; food; furniture, jobs.

Variation

The game known as 'The Vicar's Cat' can be adapted to incorporate clapping quite easily. Each student fits a whole sentence into the rhythm:

'The Vicar's cat is a(n) __________ cat.'
[clap] [clap] [click] [click]

Each student uses a different adjective in the blank space.

1.11 Commentary

Language Narrative tenses

Level Intermediate–Advanced

Age Any

Procedure

1. Choose a group of two or three 'storytellers'. These can be swapped during the course of the activity to give everyone a chance to narrate. The rest of the class act as 'performers'. Give the storytellers the beginning of a story. For example:

   'John had been waiting for Rachel for an hour.'

2. As you say this, choose a 'John' from the assembled performers. He mimes waiting and impatience.
3. The storytellers now continue the story a sentence at a time, and see it performed in front of them by the rest of the class. This creation of a visual aspect of their story should act as a stimulus for imaginative language use.

Variation

Do this the other way round: the performers do a mime, and the storytellers have to do a running commentary. Whereas the main activity gives students practice in listening to each other (like an informal listening comprehension), this variation gives them the opportunity to practise describing events – which will probably provide a good opportunity for vocabulary learning and revision.

As students get used to this activity, the performers will realise that their actions need to be clearer, and the storytellers will realise that they have the freedom to place new interpretations on what they see.

Notes

This is mime! Props are not only unnecessary, but they get in the way. Imagination can be a more powerful tool if there is no realism to prevent its development.

You might also wish to forbid physical contact between performers. Fight scenes, for example, can be very amusing if touching is not allowed. They are also less dangerous this way!

You might need to prompt the storytellers occasionally (without taking their story over completely), or you could swap a storyteller for a performer if ideas begin to run dry. You will probably also be needed to allocate characters to performers as the story goes on.

1.12 Conditional string

Language 1st and 2nd conditionals

Level Intermediate–Advanced

Age Any

Procedure

1. This can be done in a fixed sequence like a 'circle' exercise. The teacher begins with a conditional sentence:

   'If I won the lottery, I'd buy a yacht.'

2. The next person in the sequence then changes the 'would' part of the sentence to a new 'if' clause:

   'If I bought a yacht, . . .'

   and finishes the sentence in a suitable manner:

   '. . . I'd sail to Australia.'

3. This continues around the class with as much speed as possible.

> *Possible opening sentences:*
>
> 'If I won the lottery, I'd have a lot of money.'
> 'If I became president, I'd be in charge of the country.'
> 'If I met a genie, I'd have three wishes.'
> 'If I moved abroad, I'd live in France.'
> 'If I was richer, I'd buy a new house.'

Extension

Students could be encouraged to use the 1st and 2nd conditionals according to how likely they feel the events which they suggest are:

'If I bought a new house, I'd get a pet dog.'
'If I get a pet dog, I'll go for more walks.'
'If I go for more walks, I'll lose some weight.'
etc.

The exercise could then be used to introduce the differences between conditional types, and extended to serve as early practice in these structures.

1.13 Debates

Language All

Level Intermediate–Advanced

Age Young adult upwards

The principles of debating are well-known, with participants putting forward deliberately conflicting views on a topic to inspire speeches and discussion. The largest problem facing their use in the language classroom is motivation. If students share the same first language, then anything of vital importance is likely to be discussed – naturally enough – in their native language rather than in the target language. Anything of less importance is liable to run out of steam after a few minutes.

Procedure

One solution to this is to reduce debates to simple 'brainstorming' sessions, followed by a vote. For example, the teacher might ask the class what the advantages and disadvantages of a proposition could be. A simple vote to decide if the proposition is acceptable is taken when all possibilities have been exhausted.

Propositions for brainstorming advantages and disadvantages:

More people should learn Spanish.
Smoking should be banned.
Water should be rationed.
Soft drugs should be made legal.
TV should be banned for under-16s.
All cars should run on electricity.
Unhealthy food should be taxed.
Everyone should use the same currency.
Parents should need a 'child licence'.
Students should be able to 'sack' teachers.

Variation for adult students

Many adults, however, will enjoy the opportunity to practise their public speaking skills, so a topic for a short presentation could be set for homework. In class, the other students could then comment on how the presentation could have been improved, could provide 'questions to the speaker', or could make an opposing presentation.

To inspire discussion, students could be asked to prepare presentations which have contrasting titles. These will depend on the needs and interests of individual students, and only the teacher 'on the spot' is in a position to judge whether topics are likely to be successful or not.

Contrasting presentations to prepare for homework:

1. Not enough people are learning English.
   Too many people are learning English.
   English is the most difficult language to learn.
2. Corporal punishment in schools is necessary.
   Corporal punishment in schools is unnecessary.
   Corporal punishment in schools is wrong.

1.14 Designs

Language Describing things

Level Intermediate–Advanced

Age Any

Procedure

Think of a common, household object with which everyone in the class is familiar (for example, a bed). Ask the class to tell you what they like and dislike most about this object. Then ask them to think of the most luxurious ways to improve the object.

Allow imagination. Beds with overhead video machines and built-in drinks cabinets are quite acceptable. But also be practical: Where are the controls for the video? How is the drinks cabinet opened?

Rationale

The advantage of doing this orally is that students who are not good at drawing do not feel inhibited from adding something simply because it is difficult to draw. Sometimes a lack of resources can be turned to your linguistic advantage!

> *Other household objects to design:*
> (These should be suitable for use in most cultures.)
>
> Baths/showers, chairs, cooking facilities, cupboards, doors, garden tools, sheds for pets or other animals, tables, windows.

Variation

Ask students to describe the cheapest, most environmentally friendly way to make your household object.

Classes have been known to describe beds made of old rags and dried cow dung . . .

1.15 Fizz buzz

Language Sounds, numbers

Level Beginner–Elementary

Age Children

This is an old counting game which can be used as a 'circle' exercise.

Procedure

1. Around the 'circle' students count upwards from one, each student saying one number. However, if a number is divisible by three, they say 'fizz' instead of the number. The sequence would begin:

   'one, two, fizz, four, five, fizz, seven, eight, fizz, ten'

2. Continue until each student has had two or three turns, or until there is little hesitation and few mistakes.

Variations

i) Insert a different word for all multiples of 3 *and* 5 (or any other two small numbers you choose), so that if a number is divisible by 3, students say 'fizz', and if it is divisible by 5, they say 'buzz'. Counting from one to ten would then produce the sequence:

'one, two, fizz, four, buzz, fizz, seven, eight, fizz, buzz'

The number fifteen would be 'fizz buzz'.

ii) Students say every number plus the relevant additions, so three would be 'three fizz', fifteen would be 'fifteen fizz buzz', and so on. The advantage of this variation is that students actively practise the number system as well as the phonetic system of the target language.

iii) 'Fizz' and 'buzz' are replaced by more common English words, for example 'stand' and 'sit'. Young learners might enjoy actually performing these actions each time the word is said. This also introduces more energy into the learning situation.

1.16 Guessing games I

Language Simple questions

Level Elementary upwards

Age Any

There are many guessing games based on the concept of one person 'knowing', and the rest of the class 'guessing'. These all involve 'yes/no' questions.

I-spy

This involves the 'knower' giving the first letter of an object he or she can see, and the rest guessing what it is. Each puzzle traditionally begins with the form 'I spy, with my little eye, something beginning with A.', where 'A' becomes the student's chosen letter.

Twenty questions

Also known as 'Animal, vegetable, mineral,' this involves providing the category of an object, which is one of the three headings given above. The guessing students are then given twenty attempts to learn something about the object before they have to guess what it is. More advanced learners might include the fourth option of 'Abstract' for nouns of emotion, and so on.

The coffee-pot game

This is also frequently used in many language classrooms, and can target any grammatical category, although verbs are particularly suitable. In each question the word 'coffee-pot' is used instead of the word which the questioner is trying to guess (and which the 'knower' might have written down on a piece of paper). This leads to questions such as:

> 'Do you coffee-pot every morning?'
> 'Do you coffee-pot with friends?', and so on.

Other objects which can be identified using 'yes/no' questioning include:

Animals; classroom objects; countries or languages; famous people; food; jobs; tools.

Note

These games function better as language-learning aids if you encourage information-finding questions. Guessing classroom objects, for example, can be very unproductive with a constant stream of 'Is it a table?', 'Is it a textbook?', and so on. It might be worth limiting teams to only three 'direct' guesses per item, thus encouraging different types of question.

See also the activities 'Anagrams' (2.1), 'Hangman' (2.8) and 'Picture it' (2.10).

1.17 Guessing games II

Language All

Level Elementary upwards

Age Any

Procedure

The second major type of guessing game places greater emphasis on giving information rather than eliciting information. Traditionally the 'knower' gives the class a sentence about the object or person, and the class guesses once between sentences. To reduce the responsibility placed on individual 'knowers', however, this can also be done with one or two students as 'guessers', and the rest of the class giving them information.

Example sentences giving clues about 'Clint Eastwood', under the category 'Famous people' might be:

> 'He talks very quietly.'
> 'He often wears a hat and smokes.'
> 'He can be a cowboy or a policeman.'
> 'Some people say he is "dirty".'

Variation for large classes

In large classes students could be divided into competing teams, which could consult after receiving each fresh piece of information and take turns at guessing each other's words.

Useful topics here would be:

Famous people	(Clues: looks, routines, achievements)
Films and plays	(Clues: plot and setting)
Sports and games	(Clues: rules and equipment)
Advertisements	(Clues: setting, words – story and music if it is on radio or TV)

Note

Obviously the clue sentences should not be too explicit. The advantage of a competitive situation, where the 'knowers' give clues to an opposing team, is that this encourages participants to be more vague, which stretches the imagination a little more. But of course no lying is allowed!

1.18 Guess the story

Language Simple questions

Level Intermediate–Advanced

Age Any

There are many short stories which can be used for a guessing game such as this. Some possible sources are listed in the bibliography at the back of this book. Alternatively, you could use interesting news items or magazine articles.

Procedure

Give the class two or three clue words taken from the story. The class then asks 'yes/no' questions to try to discover from you what the story is. If necessary a time limit or a maximum number of questions can be set before the class attempts to recreate the story for themselves, which they do orally. Only answer questions which are correctly formed.

Example

Here is one example story, adapted from a real news bulletin. It is suitable for upper intermediate students:

> *Clue words:* India, meditation, salary.
>
> An Indian man was having some bad luck, and had lost nearly all his money. He decided to write to a famous Englishman to ask him for some money so that he could reverse his fortunes.
>
> Some time later, the Englishman wrote back, saying: 'all things are possible through meditation'.
>
> This did not help the Indian very much.
>
> However, when the Englishman died some years later, the Indian sold the note which he had been sent. The price was double his annual salary!
>
> (In the real story, the Englishman was John Lennon.)

Variation

In *Grammar Games*, Mario Rinvolucri suggests a similar exercise, but done in silence with students taking turns to write questions on the blackboard. If you have a blackboard, this provides a very useful focus on the grammar of simple questions.

1.19 I can I can't

Language 'Can/can't'

Level Elementary–Intermediate

Age Any

This is best done in small, fast-moving groups (or circles) of between six and eight people. So if your class is larger, do one test run with the whole class, and then divide the class into groups.

Procedure

Tell the person on your left something which you can do:

> 'I can swim.'

The sentence 'travels' all the way around the class with students using 'can/can't' as appropriate to themselves. The objective is to find as many things as possible which everyone in the group can or can't do.

Variations

i) This is also a useful exercise for introducing the present perfect tense as an expression of experience. Start with a sentence such as:

> 'I've been to Canada.'

The objective is then to find things which either everybody or nobody in the group has done.

ii) Start the activity the same way, telling the person on your left something which you can do:

> 'I can drive a car.'

In this version, however, all 'can' sentences go clockwise, and all 'can't' sentences go anti-clockwise. Therefore if the student can also do this thing, he or she repeats the same sentence to the next person in the sequence, and so on. If they can't, they say back to you:

'I can't drive a car.'

No person is allowed to use the same main verb twice, so you must then think of something you can't do and tell this to the person on your right, i.e. the next person anti-clockwise in the sequence:

'I can't speak Italian.'

They either continue anti-clockwise with the same sentence, or, if they *can* speak Italian, they return it to you as a new 'I can' construction.

By changing the direction of the sequence as indicated, the opposite nature of 'can' and 'can't' is reinforced for students. The objective now is to find verbs which can travel all the way round the circle in either direction.

1.20 Improv

Language All

Level Intermediate–Advanced

Age All

In activities such as 'Hats' (5.3) and 'Commentary' (1.11), students become familiar with the idea of improvising language. As spontaneity and invention are important parts of authentic language use, why not set up a full improvisation?

One good way of ensuring that an improvisation scene doesn't 'run dry' is to keep on injecting new characters or events which create a conflict of interests or beliefs. Here is one example called 'Bus stop'.

Procedure

1. Assign Student A the role of waiting for a bus. Whisper to Student B that the person waiting for a bus is actually mad, and that he or she is really standing in the middle of Student B's kitchen. Without using physical contact, Student B must get Student A to leave the kitchen.

2. The teacher then gradually introduces more characters: somebody waiting for a train; a psychiatrist who believes all the others are patients in a hospital; a cleaner trying to mop the kitchen floor; a film director and camera crew trying to record the events for a television documentary. Anything to get the students involved in the situation developing around them. The result should be a dynamic collection of simultaneous and unique interactions in the target language.
3. You can use situations arising from such activities in more specialised 'one to one' improvisation scenes.

Situations which can be utilised for particular language focus:

- an improvisation of a football coach training players could be used for imperative forms;
- a scene where spies report back after a mission would bring out reported speech;
- interviews with 'famous people' are useful for question forms.

Note

Remember that you are permitted to swap 'actors' half way through a scene, allocating the same character to a different student. Doing this prevents the improvisation from going 'stale'; this is a good way to keep the whole class concentrating on the action in front of them.

Acknowledgement

There are several books outlining methods of dramatic improvisation. Keith Johnstone's *Impro*, from which the 'Bus stop' exercise is taken, is one very useful example.

1.21 Puzzle story

Language Simple questions

Level Intermediate–Advanced

Age Any

This works in the same way as 'Guess the story' (1.18). However, instead of giving students clue words from which to guess the story, they are given the situation at the end of the story as a prompt. They use this as the basis for their questions, and to decide how the situation came about.

Examples

There are several famous examples of this. Two are given here:

Clue: A dead man is found lying in the desert, completely naked, and holding a broken match. There are no footprints anywhere nearby.

Solution: The man had been travelling with friends in a hot air balloon, which had started dropping towards the desert. They tried to reduce the weight in the balloon by taking their clothes off. When this didn't work, they drew lots to select someone to jump from the balloon.
The one who drew the broken match had to jump.

Clue: Simon lives on the ninth floor of a block of flats. Every morning he takes the lift to the ground floor as he goes to work. Every evening, however, he takes the lift as far as the fifth floor and then walks the rest of the way. Why?

Solution: Simon is very short, and cannot reach the button to take him up to the ninth floor in the lift.

Note

Good sources for similar puzzles include the cases of Sherlock Holmes, and the works of Agatha Christie. See the bibliography at the end of this book.

1.22 Simon says

Language Imperatives

Level Beginner–Elementary

Age Children

This old party game can be a useful exercise for revising vocabulary with young learners.

Procedure

The teacher shouts out instructions, which should only be obeyed if they include the words 'Simon says'.

Example instructions are:

'Simon says "Raise your right hand".'
'Simon says "Hop on your left foot".'
'Touch your toes.'
'Simon says 'Kneel on one knee".'
'Turn around.'
etc.

The exercise can be competitive between teams or individuals, with the winner being the last student to get an instruction wrong. Alternatively it can be decided on a points basis (add points for each mistake: the lowest total wins).

Variations

i) Instead of using 'Simon says' as the key words to listen for, use 'please', or polite forms such as 'could you'.

ii) As you give an instruction, perform an action yourself. This action might or might not correspond with the instruction. Students should obey your words, not necessarily copy what you are doing.

iii) The class is divided into groups. Within each group students give instructions to each other, leaving the teacher free to observe and note any mistakes for later correction.

1.23 Spot the lie

Language All

Level Elementary upwards

Age Any

This activity utilises the desire to mislead, which is sometimes inherent within competitive guessing games.

Procedure

1. Teams are created, and each team is given a topic. They must then create four sentences about that topic, but one of those sentences must contain an untruth.
2. The sentences are then presented to the rest of the class, and it is the task of the other team(s) to spot exactly what the lie is, and to explain it. The response must be more exact than simply 'Sentence 3 is wrong'. For example, four sentences about the topic 'Italy' under the category heading 'countries', and at the level of an intermediate class, might be:

    1. 'This is the home of pizza.'
    2. 'Some people say this country is in the shape of a leg.'
    3. 'The national flag is red, white and blue.'
    4. 'The national sport is football.'

   Here, of course, the answer might be:

   > 'The national flag is red, white and green, so sentence 3 is not true.'

Possible category headings:

Countries; famous people; members of the class; the teacher; English grammar; stories from films or TV programmes.

Variation

To make the exercise more difficult, the guessing team(s) need not be told what category heading the topics come under.

Acknowledgement

This is based on an exercise which appears in the book *Dictation*, by Davis and Rinvolucri.

1.24 Statues

Language Vocabulary

Level Beginner–Elementary

Age Up to teenage

This can be used as first-stage practice of new vocabulary with younger learners.

Procedure

1. Choose a student to demonstrate with. Say the word 'happy' to the whole class. Now try to 'mould' the student into looking happy. Don't touch the student, but indicate by the use of your hands how you want him or her to place his or her arms, legs, body and face in a 'happy' position. Use simple language to explain your movements:

   'Lift your head a little bit.'
   'Put your hands together.'
   etc.

2. When you have finished, say the word 'happy' again, and indicate that the student now represents this word.
3. Now divide the class into two – half 'sculptors' and half 'statues'. Give each sculptor an adjective:

   Angry, sad, scared, tired, nervous, hot, cold,
   hungry, thirsty, sick, crazy, lazy, etc.

4. Each 'sculptor' chooses a 'statue' to work with, and – without touching – tries to mould him or her into a representation of their adjective.
5. When all the statues are complete, the sculptors try to guess each other's words. Then the 'statues' and 'sculptors' swap roles, and you give each pair a new adjective.
6. An extension to this exercise is provided by 'Tableaux' (1.26), which can also be used with older learners.

Variation

Another language point which can be tackled in this way is the present continuous tense. Statues are made to represent 'He is eating dinner', and so on.

Note

Although touching is not required by this exercise (and should be discouraged), in some parts of the world you might need to be wary about cultural taboos concerning close physical proximity.

1.25 String

Language Spelling

Level Elementary upwards

Age Any

This is a quick activity which can effectively be used as a 'warm-up', or as a 'loosener' between longer activities.

Procedure

The teacher starts by saying the word 'string'. Either designate students in turn, or follow a 'circle', so that each person has to think of a word which begins with the last letter of the previous word. No word may be repeated. For example:

'string – great – together – run – needle – every'

Variation

For students at an upper-intermediate or advanced level, this can be made more difficult by asking them to use the last two letters of each word. But don't begin with the word 'string'! A sequence might start:

'gr*eat*' – '*at*l*as*' – '*as*sort*ed*' – '*edit*' – '*item*' – '*em*pire'

If you get an impossible ending, start the circle again.

Note

As a great many words in English end with the letter 'e', it might be worth forbidding these. Otherwise, students will have to think of too many words which begin with 'e'.

1.26 Tableaux

Language Present perfect

Level Intermediate

Age Any

This exercise can work as an extension of 'Statues' (1.24). However, instead of a sculptor working with a single partner, a scene is devised and shown by a small group.

Procedure

Each group is given a present perfect sentence to illustrate. They then decide on a group 'statue' to represent the sentence.

Example sentences:

'A policeman has just told a group of children to stop smoking.'
'A woman has just seen two cyclists have an accident.'
'Two old friends have just met for the first time in five years.'
'A man has just had his umbrella stolen by two youths.'
'A child has just been stung by a bee.'
'A man on a train has just been caught without a ticket.'
'A waiter has just spilt soup down a customer's new suit.'

Rationale

There is no need to have a nominated sculptor in the group, although this is possible. Instead, all the members of the group contribute their ideas of what the tableau should look like. The visual aspect of the task should help each individual to focus on the meaning of the sentence which is being worked on. When all the tableaux are ready, groups try to guess each other's sentences.

Extension

The exercise can be easily and profitably extended. Ask each group to produce a different tableau showing the same people ten seconds after the moment depicted in the first tableau. They could produce a series of about five or six such tableaux, and then present them to the class in the manner of a slow motion film. The class then decides what the situation in each 'film' is, and can even be asked to provide a running 'news' commentary.

Note

Situations arising from 'Clapping story' (1.8) can provide good material for this activity.

Acknowledgement

Both this and 'Statues' (1.24) come from the work of Augusto Boal.

1.27 What use is it?

Language Modal verbs

Level Elementary upwards

Age Any

Procedure

1. Choose any familiar object, such as a pen. (You don't even have to have one available, although if you do then it can be used for demonstration.) Ask the class how this object can be used in any ways other than the conventional way.
2. You may have to give a couple of examples to get students going:

   'It could be used as a back scratcher.'
   'It might be good as a tooth-pick.'

3. Divide the class into groups, and give each group the name of one household item. They then find as many different uses for this item as possible. Encourage the use of modal verbs.

> *Examples of household items:*
> (These will probably vary between cultures.)
>
> Gloves, matchbox, cigarette, paper clips, string, key-ring, cup, bottle, knife, fork, spoon, toothbrush.

Variation

The imagination of the class can be stimulated further by presenting this activity as one entitled 'Aliens'. Tell the class that they are all from the planet Zoltan, and that they have discovered some strange objects on planet Earth, and want to know what they are used for. If you can find enough 'strange' objects, individually or in small groups students all receive an item which they then have to describe in detail. Otherwise just use the relevant vocabulary as above. Students then present their theories about the possible uses of those objects, and demonstrate what people on Earth might do with them.

If you can get hold of them, kitchen utensils such as a sieve, corkscrew, can-opener, and so on are often useful for this exercise. Be prepared to look around for any small item with strangely shaped, flexible or moving parts, as these would be quite challenging.

1.28 Why I love

Language Because

Level Intermediate–Advanced

Age Any

This is a possible follow-up to the game 'Categories' (2.2), from which the class will have provided its own vocabulary to work with, although it can also be done independently with word sets such as those given below.

Procedure

1. Using vocabulary suitable for the level of your students, give the class one word. Students then make up sentences on the model:

   'I love XXXXX because . . .'

2. Prompt each student individually, varying the words or repeating as necessary.
3. After some time, change the model sentence to 'I hate XXXXX because . . .'

> *Possible word sets*:
>
> Intermediate:
> - Countries (USA, India, Italy, England, Japan, etc.)
> - Drinks (coffee, tea, milk, beer, whisky, etc.)
> - Food (potatoes, rice, pizza, onions, sausages, etc.)
> - Animals (dogs, cats, rabbits, mice, goldfish, parrots, etc.)
>
> Upper intermediate:
> - Famous people (chosen according to whom students are likely to have heard of: film stars, sports stars and writers, for example)
> - School subjects (geography, history, biology, French, art, etc.)
> - Festivals or events (according to local custom)
>
> Advanced:
> - Types of television (comedy, soaps, news, sports, etc., or specific programmes)
> - Types of music (pop, classical, rap, rock and roll etc., or specific songs or groups)
> - Spare time activities (walking, fishing, shopping, reading, doing homework, watching TV, etc.)

2 Activities using blackboard only

2.1 Anagrams

Language Vocabulary sets

Level Elementary–Intermediate

Age Any

Anagram puzzles are a good way of reinforcing newly presented vocabulary. Usually they are set by the teacher, but teams can set the questions for each other. In this case, to save time, the clues do not necessarily have to be real 'anagrams' – rearranging the letters of individual words is sufficient.

Procedure

Compile a list of about ten anagrams using words from your chosen vocabulary set. Write these anagrams on the board, and set a time limit for groups to try to discover *all* the answers. Emphasise that you will not accept answers to individual questions.

Example 'food words' for intermediate level:

Anagrams	**Jumbled words**
cheap (peach)	hfsi (fish)
lump (plum)	gaseuas (sausage)
untape (peanut)	annaab (banana)
tap too (potato)	enhyo (honey)
no rage (orange)	idgudpn (pudding)
mad rust (mustard)	riglac (garlic)
cool cheat (chocolate)	hugtroy (yoghurt)
of feet (toffee)	cluttee (lettuce)
plain peep (pineapple)	telemote (omelette)
weds chains (sandwiches)	mottoa (tomato)

Extension

When groups have solved the puzzles, and you have gone through the answers, see how many more items students can add to your list in the given topic.

Variation for advanced students

For more advanced classes, it is also possible to introduce idioms using anagrams or jumbled words. Select one or two words of the idiom, and make those into puzzles to solve. Students then try to explain the meaning of the idiom as a whole.

> *Example idiom puzzles:*
>
> 'As fit as a *fed lid*' (fiddle)
> 'As clean as a *he wilts*' (whistle)
> '*This cat* in time *vases* nine' (A stitch / saves)
> 'Kill *word bits* with *noose ten*' (two birds / one stone)

2.2 Categories

Language Vocabulary sets

Level Elementary upwards

Age Any

Procedure

1. Divide the class into teams of about 5–6 students. Write the following categories on the blackboard:

   Countries
   Food
   Jobs
   Animals
   Furniture
   Clothing
   Colours

2. Then give the class a letter (for example, 'G'). Each team must think of one word from each category which begins with that letter.
3. After a time – say, ten minutes – check the words. Teams only score a point if no other team has thought of their word.
4. A possible follow-up to this, using the vocabulary which has been identified, would be the activity 'Why I love' (1.28).

2.3 Class story

Language Narrative forms

Level Elementary upwards

Age Any

This is a good interactive way of providing a model composition before asking students to do a similar one for individual homework. It can also be used for consolidating language points which have been covered in class.

Procedure

1. Simply give the class a title at the top of the blackboard, and invite suggestions:

   'How should the story be started?'
   'What should the next sentence be?'
   'What should the characters be called?'
   'What should happen next?'

2. The class must decide collectively at each point on the best way to proceed, and the teacher writes the resulting story on the board, correcting grammar as appropriate. Encourage the use of past tenses and reported speech.
3. At the end, select one member of the class to read the story aloud. This allows the class to see the pattern of the whole text, and to feel more easily where the individual sentences which they have been working on fit into this framework.

Variation

This is also a good exercise for introducing or revising the conventions of letter writing. Make sure that students know where to put addresses, the date, and greetings, and that they know how to sign off at the end. Check that students can identify the differences between formal and informal language.

2.4 Cross words

Language Vocabulary definitions

Level Intermediate–Advanced

Age Any

Procedure

1. On the left half of the blackboard draw an empty crossword grid of about ten spaces by ten spaces, and then write 'CROSSWORD' along the top row of the grid:

C	R	O	S	S	W	O	R	D	■

2. Check that students know the rules of crosswords – particularly that two letters cannot be next to each other unless they form a word – and then ask them to suggest words which could fit into the grid. Begin with words coming down from the letters which you have already put in.
3. Discourage words of three letters or less until you are filling in the spaces at the end.
4. When you have sufficient words (about twelve), number them according to normal crossword procedure – numbering from the top, moving horizontally from left to right.

5. Now ask the class what a crossword is. They might say something like 'A word game'. So, on the right side of the board, write:

   'ACROSS: 1. A word game.'

6. Continue with the other words in the crossword until you have definitions for all of them.

Follow up

If you have paper and pens available, possible follow-up exercises to this include:

i) Have each student create their own crossword grid and clues for homework. In class they then try to solve each other's puzzles.

ii) Copy the class crossword onto paper, then onto the blackboard for another class to solve. Don't help students too much. It could be possible to have an 'exchange' system of puzzles between classes.

2.5 Doodles

Language Modal verbs

Level Elementary–Intermediate

Age Any

This works in much the same way as 'Draw and describe' (2.6), but relies more heavily on imagination.

Procedure

1. The teacher draws a series of 'doodles' (lines and swirls, or mixtures of geometric shapes, similar to those below – any pattern will do), and then encourages the class to suggest what the patterns 'could' or 'might' represent.
2. Try to elicit quite detailed answers. For example, if someone suggests an animal, find out where in the drawing the animal's eyes, tail, nose, and so on are. Find out what the animal is doing. Activate as much language as possible.
3. You might like to take a class vote to decide what each object really is!

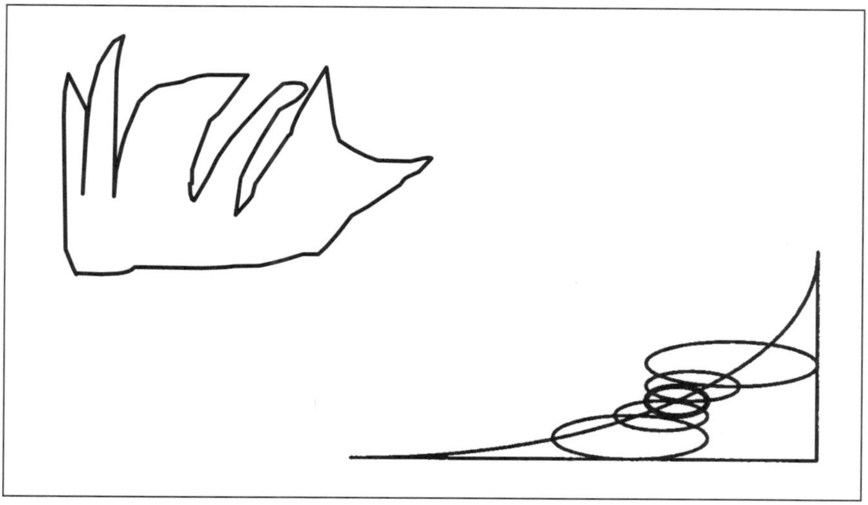

Variation

Instead of the teacher drawing the 'doodles', this job can be given to members of the class.

2.6 Draw and describe

Language Describing objects; present continuous

Level Elementary–Intermediate

Age Any

As well as its use for teaching the language points above, this is a good exercise to use as an informal needs analysis at the beginning of the first lesson with a new class of non-beginners.

Procedure

1. Silently draw a simple picture of a small house in the centre of the blackboard. Pass the chalk to a student, and indicate that they should add something to the picture. In turn, every student in the class is then given an opportunity to contribute to the drawing,

which should help to get them personally involved in the following language activity.

2. When the picture is complete, begin to elicit language. Begin with simple questions such as 'What is it?' and 'What is happening here?' to describe explicit points about the picture. If the class is sufficiently good, you can then go on to more complicated questions, such as 'What do you think has just happened?', or 'What is going to happen next?', or 'Why is that happening?'. Together, these questions should be sufficient to produce enough language to give the teacher quite a good idea of the ability of the students.

Variations

i) The silent period in this exercise works with a new class because it helps them to relax into a strange situation. With familiar or more confident classes, each individual student can describe what they are drawing as they draw it. The whole class is then encouraged to move on to the speculative questions as above.

ii) Instead of each individual thinking of something to draw, the rest of the class makes suggestions and the student with the chalk chooses the 'best' one.

2.7 Fathers and daughters

Language Complaints; questions

Level Intermediate–Advanced

Age Young adult upwards

Procedure

1. Write a list of relatives across the top of the blackboard:

   'father – mother – daughter – son – sister – brother'

2. Give the class an example of a real personal complaint:

   'I don't like it when my mother . . .'
   'I wish my father wouldn't . . .'
   'If only my son would . . .'

3. Elicit more such complaints about members of their families from

the class. Write the best of these on the blackboard. When you have a good selection of complaints, divide the class into groups. Each group then chooses one of the complaints and exemplifies it with a short role-play. You will probably need to help groups with this. Give them example situations if they are struggling, for example:

> 'A daughter comes home after midnight to find mother and father waiting.'

4. Each group then performs its role-play, and after each performance the rest of the class questions the characters:

> 'Why did you [the mother] get so angry?'

5. After the question and answer session, the whole class helps the group to 'rewrite' the role-play as if the situation had occurred within a perfect family. The new role-play is performed for the whole class.

Notes

To depersonalise any criticism, it is worth trying to keep students in their roles as much as possible during the exercise, but if they wish to say something as themselves, don't forbid it.

If you have a class with a wide age-range, try to ensure that older people play younger roles, and vice versa.

With more advanced classes, the material produced by this exercise can often be used for further discussion. Which problems are the most common? How can these problems be dealt with?

It is also worth remembering that in some cultures, tackling issues such as family relationships can be a very sensitive matter.

Acknowledgement

This exercise is adapted from the work of Augusto Boal, the Brazilian theatre director who devised the 'Theatre of the Oppressed'. Details of this and other similar activities are in his book *Games for Actors and Non-Actors*.

2.8 Hangman

Language Vocabulary and spelling

Level Elementary upwards

Age Any

This traditional guessing game needs very little introduction, as it has a counterpart in many cultures. It is probably best used to review recently introduced vocabulary sets.

Procedure

One student thinks of a word, and draws a short line on the board for each letter of that word, thus indicating how many letters are in that word. The other students try to guess the individual letters of the word. Each time they guess wrongly, a section is added to a simple picture of a hanging man. If this picture is completed, the man 'hangs' and the guessing students have lost the game.

One suggested picture which 'hangs' a man after 11 wrong guesses is:

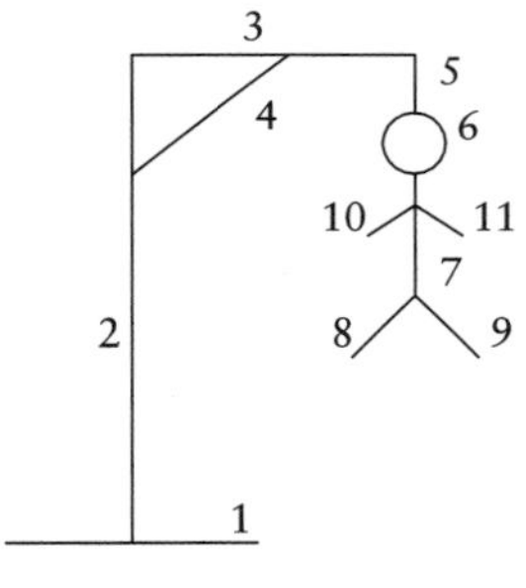

Over-complicated pictures are not recommended!

Note

Some points need to be emphasised for this to work efficiently in the language classroom, however. Using small teams in a competitive situation involves a larger proportion of the class in active thought. It is also a good idea to consider the following, and make these points clear before beginning the game:

- What is the exact picture required to 'hang' the man?
- What is the topic for the vocabulary being used?
- Is there a time limit for guessing words?

Another possibility is to appoint a 'speaker' from each team to avoid the chaos of everyone making guesses at the same time.

> *Possible topics include*:
>
> Animals, countries, food, names of films, parts of the body, school subjects, sports, types of building or transport.

2.9 Letters

Language Vocabulary

Level Elementary upwards

Age Any

Procedure

1. Tell the class that they are going to choose eight letters by telling you eight numbers between 1 and 99. Explain that odd numbers represent consonants, and even numbers represent vowels.
2. As the students choose their eight numbers, use the chart below to 'translate' the numbers into letters, which you then write on the board. Remember not to let the students see the chart. Each number may be used only once per game. For example, the numbers 7, 12, 95 would, on this chart, produce the letters T, U, S.

	0	1	2	3	4	5	6	7	8	9
00	■	G	O	L	I	P	A	T	U	K
10	O	N	U	S	E	Y	I	R	A	W
20	E	K	U	M	U	R	U	C	E	T
30	U	B	O	T	A	S	E	D	I	L
40	A	T	E	F	O	Z	O	W	A	N
50	U	Q	A	C	E	J	E	T	O	H
60	E	S	A	Y	O	G	I	B	U	X
70	O	H	I	R	I	F	O	L	E	C
80	I	L	E	W	A	V	A	P	O	Y
90	A	P	I	D	U	S	E	N	I	S

3. When you have all eight letters on the board, set a time limit (about a minute), and students try to find the longest word possible using only the given letters, and without repeating any – as for an anagram.

Variation

Write a long English word (maybe 'INTERNATIONAL') on the blackboard. Students are given a time limit, in which they must try to produce as many words of more than three letters as possible, using only the letters in this word.

Acknowledgement

This idea is based on the Channel 4 television programme 'Countdown'.

2.10 Picture it

Language Vocabulary

Level Intermediate

Age Any

Procedure

Have a number of words, phrases, idioms or situations ready to give to students (either written on cards or just ready to whisper to individuals). If you do this exercise with idioms, it is especially important that these should be taken from material which you have taught recently, otherwise they will be unguessable. Give one student the first item, and then – without speaking or using written words – this student must try to represent it in picture form on the blackboard. The rest of the class tries to guess what the drawing represents.

Variations

i) If you have no blackboard, this can be done as a version of the mime game 'Charades', with students acting out each phrase or situation to be guessed. In this case, it is probably best to tell the class the topic of the word or situation to be guessed.

Examples:

Intermediate words: Bottle-opener; breakfast; disco; ghosts; jelly; marmalade; moonlight; opera; poetry; shampoo; yoghurt; x-ray.
Upper-intermediate words: Alien; assassin; curry; egg yolk; examination; forbidden; hypnotist; marathon; mosquito; nail varnish; nightmare; pick-pocket; tobacco; whipped cream.

Intermediate idioms/phrases: Asking for trouble; catch a cold; dressed to kill; fed up; getting down to business; going nowhere fast; many hands make light work.
Upper-intermediate idioms/phrases: Barking up the wrong tree; beating about the bush; doing time; having a ball; jumping to conclusions; kill two birds with one stone; a rolling stone gathers no moss; a stitch in time saves nine.

Intermediate situations: Catching a bus; baking a cake; doing the shopping; going to the dentist; having a geography lesson; having a picnic; Saturday afternoon; visiting the zoo in the rain.
Upper-intermediate situations: Arriving at a party; giving a speech at a wedding; making a salad; making the bed. (If teaching English for Specific or Professional Purposes, make this list according to student needs. Medical English, for example, might include dressing a wound or giving an injection.)

ii) Separate the class into two teams. Each team then makes a list of phrases or situations which the other team has to work on according to the rules of the game, i.e. with one of the teams drawing or miming and the others guessing. The team which guesses the most items correctly is the winner.

Acknowledgement

This is based on the well-known game 'Pictionary'.

2.11 Ratings

Language Comparatives

Level Intermediate–Advanced

Age Any

Procedure

1. Choose a type of equipment, such as 'drawing materials', and make a list of five or six things which fit into this category. Write these down the left hand side of the blackboard, and complete the chart like the one below:

	Efficiency	*Looks*	*Value*	*Versatility*
Pencil and paper Chalk and slate Ink, quill and paper Computer and printer Oil paint and canvas Wax crayon and card				

2. The class now has to agree on a rating of 1–5 for each item under each heading. So an item which the class thinks is extremely efficient, very attractive to look at, excellent value for money, and capable of a wide range of uses, will score 5 under each heading: a total of 20 points. As students decide the ratings, encourage them to compare the numbers given for each item. This part of the discussion will then provide the most effective practice in the use of comparatives, so try to make sure that as many students as possible take an active part in the decision making. Ideally, everyone in the class should agree on each number given, but as in large classes this is often impractical, you might have to ask students to make some compromises.
3. Add up the totals for each item, and put them into order. Ask the class if they agree with the order which has been produced. If not, where did the analysis go wrong?

Other possible types of equipment:

timepieces (wristwatch, grandfather clock, Big Ben, alarm clock, etc.)
drinking vessels (teacup, wine glass, paper cup, coconut shell, etc.)
transport (jumbo jet, submarine, bicycle, skis, etc.)
hats (bowler hat, sou'wester, beret, policeman's helmet, etc.)

Note

If necessary, the initial rating part of the exercise can be done in groups, and the different results brought together and compared. A set of class ratings is then agreed. It is, of course, also possible to change the criteria according to which items are rated. Types of clothing, for example, might be rated according to how 'comfortable', 'economical', 'fashionable' and 'practical' they are.

2.12 Self questioning

Language Question forms

Level Elementary upwards

Age Any

This is a simple exercise, but an effective teaching method nevertheless, as it makes the language which learners produce directly relevant to them.

Procedure

Give the class a topic such as 'holidays'. (Choose the topic according to the needs and weaknesses of the individuals involved.) Orally, students then 'brainstorm' questions which they could ask someone who has just come back from holiday:

'Where did you go?'
'What was the weather like?'
etc.

You can write these questions on the board yourself, or get a 'secretary' from the class to do it for you. When you have a good selection of grammatically correct questions written on the board, use these to ask the students themselves about their last holiday (or whatever the chosen topic is).

Suggested topics:

Ambitions, dreams, family and friends, food and cooking, holidays, jobs, journeys, music, parties, pets, school lessons or exams, shopping, sports, weekend and spare time activities.

Extension

If you are teaching EAP (English for Academic Purposes) or ESP (English for Specific Purposes), this is a good exercise for potential interviewers. It could lead in to a discussion about 'What makes a good question?'.

2.13 Sentence anagrams

Language Word order

Level Elementary upwards

Age Any

This exercise builds on the idea of 'Anagrams' (2.1), but focuses on the grammar of sentences rather than the spelling of vocabulary.

Preparation

In preparation, write a sentence suitable for the language point which you are dealing with, and 'shuffle' the words around. For example, a lesson on phrasal verbs might include a sentence such as:

> 'He picked English up easily, but German was getting him down.'

You could mix this up to become:

> 'English, German, up, down, he, him, getting, easily, but, picked, was.'

Procedure

Write these words on the blackboard (or dictate them if this suits your situation better). The class then attempts to make a good English sentence using only those words. As the aim of this exercise is to raise awareness of acceptable word ordering within sentences, accept any grammatically correct sentence, even if it is different from your original.

Variation

To take the 'anagram' idea another step up the language ladder, it can also be adapted for 'paragraph anagrams' in the form of a 'Shuffled story'. Choose a reasonably long paragraph of text, and divide it into sections – either clauses or whole sentences. Mix these up and either dictate them to the class, or give one sentence to each student to dictate to the others. Then ask the class to recreate the paragraph with the sentences in the correct order.

Many cultures have a tradition of stories which involve three friends being placed in an unusual situation, and which result in the third friend doing something stupid or extraordinary. These stories often provide suitably structured material for an exercise like this. If such a formula is familiar to the students, then after the example has been solved, they can be put into groups to create new puzzles which are then dictated for the other groups to work on. An example for the teacher to start with is given below.

Example 'Shuffled story' (with the sentences in the correct order):

1. Three sailors were shipwrecked on a desert island.
2. One day they found an old lamp hidden in the bushes.
3. When they started to clean it, a genie appeared
4. and granted each of the sailors one wish.
5. The first sailor thought carefully, and said
6. 'I want to be at home with my wife and children.'
7. Instantly, he disappeared in a puff of smoke.
8. The second sailor said the same thing.
9. He too disappeared from the island.
10. The third sailor thought more carefully.
11. Finally he reached a decision, and said to the genie
12. 'I want my friends back.'

Further sources for texts which can be used in this way are indicated in the Bibliography at the end of the book.

2.14 Sentence games

Language All

Level Elementary upwards

Age Any

There are many possibilities for exploring and discovering the 'rules' of language which are based on the idea of altering an existing sentence. Three of the most effective are given here.

Adding words

1. The teacher writes a simple sentence on the blackboard: maybe something like 'It is Saturday'. One by one, students must then suggest one or two words which can be added to the sentence.
2. The new words are written in, and the student who suggested the word(s) reads the new sentence aloud. The class then decides if this sentence is grammatically correct.
3. Alternatively, the teacher can indicate a place in the sentence where the new word(s) should be added, and invites suggestions from the class as a whole.

Example sequence of sentences:

'It is Saturday.'
'It is now Saturday.'
'It is now Saturday night.'
'I know it is now Saturday night.'
'I know it is now no longer Saturday night.'
etc.

Removing words

1. Using a longer starting sentence (see below for an example), students remove words singly or in pairs to make the sentence shorter. The new sentence is read aloud and a decision taken by the class as in 'Adding words' above. If the 'new' sentence is incorrect, then put back the words which had been removed.
2. This is continued until only one or two words remain in the sentence.

Changing words

Words from the teacher's original sentence can be replaced with one or two different words to change the sentence completely. The meaning of the sentence can change, but it should always be grammatically correct. Eventually every word in the sentence should be different from the original.

As above, each time a change is made, the sentence is read aloud and a class decision taken about its correctness. This is slightly different from a substitution drill such as 'Change it' (1.4), because here each word is changed only once, with the aim of creating a totally new sentence. Even the 'grammar' words such as 'and', 'was' and 'that' are replaced.

Example sentence for 'Removing words' or 'Changing words'

The patient, thinking that the examination was over, started to look for his hat; he reached out, took hold of his wife's head and tried to lift it and put it on.

(adapted from Oliver Sacks: *The Man Who Mistook His Wife For A Hat*)

Note

The bibliography at the end of this book contains some ideas for finding other suitable sentences to work with.

Acknowledgement

These and many similar ideas are presented in Mario Rinvolucri's book *Grammar Games*. In turn, a lot of these come from the principles of 'The Silent Way' teaching methods.

2.15 Silent story

Language Narrative forms

Level Elementary upwards

Age Any

Procedure

1. As with 'Class story' (2.3), write the title of a composition at the top of the blackboard. This time, however, also write the first three words of the story: maybe 'There was once'.
2. In silence, each member of the class comes up to the blackboard and adds three words to the story. Be strict about the number of words each student is allowed per visit, and include 'a' and 'an' in the word count.

Note

By *not* writing a title for the class at the beginning of the exercise, you can leave the decision-making entirely in their hands. Ask students to provide a title after the story has been written.

2.16 Word change

Language Vocabulary and spelling

Level Intermediate–Advanced

Age Any

Procedure

Divide the class into teams of about 5–6 students. Write a four-letter word on the board, for example 'BEAN'. Each team elects a scribe, and the teams take it in turns to tell their scribe a new word to write underneath the previous one. Each new word must change only one letter from the word which went before, and no repeats are allowed.

One sequence, for example, might be:

'bean – bear – beer – deer – deep' – etc.

Any team unable to provide a suitable word loses points. When no team can suggest a word, start again with a new beginning.

Variation for advanced students

More advanced classes can be asked to produce words with five letters, although in this case they might need to change two letters of the word each time.

3 Activities using pens and paper only

3.1 Bingo

Language Numbers

Level Beginner–Elementary

Age Any

This is a good, fast, competitive game to concentrate students' attention on listening to you in English (or other target language). Remember, however, to keep the rules as simple as possible.

Procedure

1. For a quick game, don't use a wide range of numbers. Each student chooses five numbers between 1 and 30, and writes them down.
2. Privately write down your own bingo grid as below – or simply list the numbers 1–30. Choose numbers randomly, call out a different number about every five seconds or so, and cross it off your grid. Don't repeat each call more than once, or students lose the need to listen.

1	2	3	4	5	6
7	8	9	10	11	12
13	14	15	16	17	18
19	20	21	22	23	24
25	26	27	28	29	30

3. When a student has heard all his or her numbers called, he or she shouts 'Bingo!'. Check the student's numbers against the ones you have crossed off your own grid, and, if you can, give a small prize to the winner.

Variation

This game can also be played using a set of words. Irregular past tenses are a good example, but any set of recently learned vocabulary can be used if it can be accurately defined within similar 'limits'.

3.2 Chinese whispers

Language Pronunciation

Level Intermediate–Advanced

Age Any

Also known as 'The broken telephone', this is an old party game that is well suited to lines, rows or circles of students working as teams. Groups of about ten are ideal, so it is particularly good for large classes.

Procedure

1. Find a text of suitable difficulty (an example for upper-intermediate students is given below, while sources for other texts can be found in the bibliography at the end of of this book), and split it into sections. Divide the class into groups, making sure that the students in each group are placed in a set sequence.
2. Whisper the first line of the text to a representative from each group. They memorise it, and whisper it to the next person in their group, and so on along the line or around the circle. When they are ready, the representatives should return to you for the next section of text. If the exercise is to be competitive, deduct points if any student other than the group representative moves out of his or her place.
3. The final student in each group writes what he or she hears on a piece of paper. At the end of the activity, read out students' versions, and then the real version.

Variation

If there is a blackboard available, the end of the exercise can be a visual grammar correction exercise using the 'new' versions as raw material. This would produce a grammatically correct, if not identical, version of the original text. If you wish, you can then compare the two versions.

Doing a correction of this sort helps students to place what they heard into a grammatical structure, without imposing a 'right' and 'wrong' text on their own creative listening.

> *Text for upper-intermediate students*:
>
> The driver relied on travel as a form of reflection,
> but the Volvo had never been out of Vermont.
> The driver was an officious traveller;
> he kept his oil up and his windshield clean
> and he carried his own tyre gauge
> in his left breast pocket
> next to a ball-point pen.
> The pen was for making entries in the Grand Trip List,
> such things as gas mileage,
> toll fees and riding time.
>
> (adapted from John Irving's 'Almost In Iowa', in *Trying To Save Piggy Sneed*)

3.3 Consequences

Language Conjunctions; reported speech

Level Elementary upwards

Age Any

This is another traditional game easily adapted to a language-learning environment. It can be done in a circle, but works equally well in rows.

Procedure

1. Each person in the circle or row has a pen and a piece of paper. Tell everyone to silently write the name of a famous person (or other person known to the whole class) at the top of the piece of paper. They then fold the paper over to hide the name, and pass it to the person next to them (on their left if they are in a circle; behind them if they are in a row – which means you will have to take the paper

from the person at the back of the row and give it to the person at the front).

2. Without unfolding the new piece of paper, students then write the name of a second person below the original fold. They fold the paper and pass it on as before.
3. Students now write what their first person said to their second person. Fold and pass. Write the reply. Fold and pass. Write what happened because of this short conversation. Fold and pass. The initial folding pattern is shown below. Continue in the same manner for all the items which students have to write on their sheets of paper.

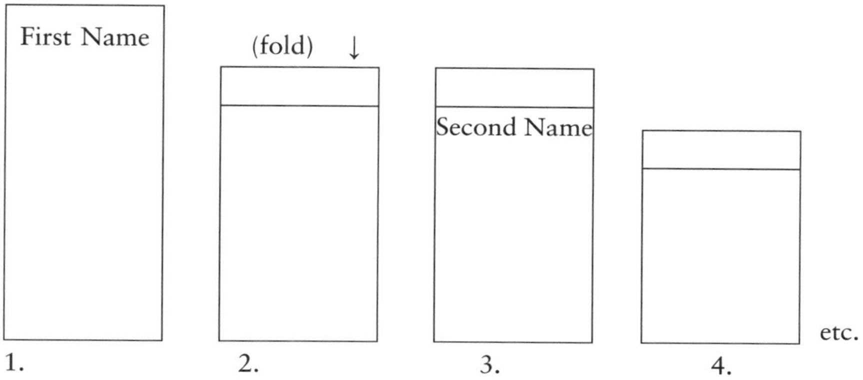

4. After the papers have been passed on for the final time, everyone unfolds the piece of paper which they have been given. They use the 'prompts' on the paper to tell or write a short story using the target language structures. It is this stage which is the most valuable for developing students' narrative skills, and especially their use of conjunctions in sequencing clauses, so the teacher should pay particular attention to these points when listening to or reading the 'compositions'.

Variation

Students write on the papers and pass them on as above, but without the folding process. This means that the final result is not so surprising, and often not so funny, but the activity as a whole focuses more on reading comprehension skills.

3.4 Definitions

Language Dictionary definitions

Level Intermediate–Advanced

Age Any

Rationale

Most students, even in limited resource communities, will need to make use of a dictionary at some point. This activity extends their appreciation of the ways a dictionary works without the necessity of having multiple dictionaries available.

Procedure

1. Depending on the size of the class, this can be done in pairs, or in groups. Give about five recently taught words to each pair or group. Students then write down a definition of each word using the target language.
2. When they finish, they read the definitions to the class; the other students try to guess the original words. In particularly large classes, groups can read definitions to each other, while the teacher circulates around the class noting mistakes for later correction.

Note

This exercise works well with vocabulary sets for less advanced students, where it can be a learning process as well as a revision tool, but more proficient classes might enjoy the challenge of having apparently random words to define.

Variation

'Call my bluff' is a similar game. Each group chooses a word which they think the other groups won't know. They then write three definitions for the word, only one of which is true. They present all three definitions to the rest of the class, which has to decide which definition is the correct one. Teams gain points for guessing correctly. The game is named after the British television series which introduced it.

3.5 Dictation

Language All

Level Elementary upwards

Age Any

The traditional dictation is still considered by many to be a useful device for English language teaching. Even with very large groups, it allows individuals to focus on grammatical structures, on the irregular spellings often found in English, and on listening comprehension techniques. In a limited-resource situation, it is also a useful method of presenting an interesting text (from a newspaper or magazine) to the class before doing further work on it.

Procedure

In its 'pure' form dictation involves the teacher reading a text three times: once at normal speed for students to hear the text as a whole; once at a slow speed so that students can write the text down; and once more at normal speed to allow students to check through what they have written.

Variations

There is, however, also a growing body of non-traditional dictation which places the focus on the meanings of individual words or sentences, rather than simply on their form. Try:

i) dictating a text with gaps, which students then have to fill in themselves;

ii) dictating single words which students then write in the most appropriate place (to them) on a picture or map which they have drawn themselves;

iii) dictating a text only at normal speed, but repeating as often as necessary so that students can pay close attention as and when they need to in order to complete their writing;

iv) giving each student a single sentence of a text to dictate to the rest of the class, which then decides on the correct order of the sentences.

Acknowledgement

These and many similar exercises can be found in Davis and Rinvolucri's book *Dictation*, listed in the bibliography at the back. This bibliography also provides possible sources for suitable dictation texts.

3.6 Giving presents

Language 'Would have' and 'because'

Level Intermediate

Age Any

Procedure

1. Each student writes his or her name on a piece of paper. All the names are then collected by the teacher.
2. Explain to the class that yesterday was a special occasion (such as the birthday of the Queen's favourite corgi!), but that you forgot. Tell students that if you had remembered, they could have given one person in the class a special present.
3. Each student then picks a piece of paper at random from those you have collected. On the back of that paper, he or she draws a picture of the present they would have given to the person named on the front. (If a student picks his or her own name, they must put it back and choose again.) Then they write an explanation:

   'I would have given Jean-Paul (a) . . . because . . .'

4. When everyone has finished, one by one students stand up, read their explanations, and give their 'presents'. In particularly large classes, a few sentences can be read as examples, and then the rest of the students can get up and move around the classroom giving their 'presents', and giving explanations to each other. The teacher can monitor this by being alert for good examples which can be repeated in front of the whole class when all the presents have been given.

Acknowledgement

This activity is adapted from an idea which I first saw in use at a British Council workshop run by Phil Dexter in Sofia, Bulgaria.

3.7 Poems alive!

Language All; pronunciation

Level Intermediate–Advanced

Age Young adult upwards

Preparation

Choose some reasonably short poems, or extracts from a longer one. Suggestions for sources can be found in the bibliography at the end of the book. Write the extracts on separate pieces of paper. One poem for every five students should be sufficient.

Procedure

In class, split the students into groups, and give each group one of the poems. Tell them they must find a way to recite and act out the poem. After a period of preparation, the poems are 'performed' in front of the whole class.

Rationale

This process of 'acting out' allows students to concentrate on the meanings of the words as well as the feeling of phonetic sounds.

The Lonely Man

He was sitting alone:
sad, weary,
with a tear-stained face.
I asked him: Why?

He looked at me silently
and kept quiet.

I asked him again: Why?
Again he looked silently
into my eyes
and said nothing.

Then he got up and went away
leaving behind his silence.

(by Omar Ali, translated
by Pritish Nandy)

Example

One poem suitable for intermediate learners is shown on the previous page.

Because they are usually written with visual considerations in mind, play extracts are also useful for this exercise. The text below could be used with an upper-intermediate or advanced class:

R: We could play at questions.
G: What good would that do?
R: Practice!
G: Statement! One-love.
R: Cheating!
G: How?
R: I hadn't started yet.
G: Statement. Two-love.
R: Are you counting that?
G: What?
R: Are you counting that?
G: Foul! No repetitions. Three-love. First game to . . .
R: I'm not going to play if you're going to be like that.
G: Whose serve?
R: Hah?
G: Foul. No grunts. Love-one.
R: Whose go?
G: Why?
R: Why not?
G: What for?
R: Foul. No synonyms! One-all.

(from Tom Stoppard: *Rosencrantz And Guildenstern Are Dead*)

If you use this particular text, students might want to try to continue Stoppard's 'questions' game!

3.8 Poetry points

Language Punctuation

Level Intermediate–Advanced

Age Young adult upwards

As with the previous activity, this exercise uses poetry to focus students' attention on meanings, but this time concentrating on individual clauses.

Preparation

Choose a poem, or part of a poem, which uses short lines and punctuation. Modern poetry often works best (if you can, look for works by Adrian Henri or Brian Patten), and two examples are given below. Alternatively, if you are brave enough, you could write your own poem to suit your students' needs.

Procedure

1. In class, dictate the poem in chunks of five words. Do not dictate any punctuation, and do not split lines up according to the sense of the poem – be strict with yourself about the 'five word' rule.
2. When you have finished, students work individually to try to punctuate the poem so that it makes sense. Use this time to move around the class and check the dictation.
3. Have a poetry 'reading' at the end of the class, and encourage students to exaggerate the pronunciation and intonation which they use. This can be wonderfully liberating, and you may be surprised at the possible variations in meaning.

Example

Here are two possible poems (with punctuation removed) which you could dictate, the first for intermediate students, and the second for upper-intermediate:

A CAT, A HORSE AND THE SUN

a cat mistrusts the sun
keeps out of its way
only where sun and shadows meet
it moves

a horse loves the sun
it basks all day
snorts
and beats its hooves

the sun likes horses
but hates cats
that is why it makes hay
and heats tin rooves

(by Roger McGough)

(from) FISHERMEN

the fishermen are patient
their lines settle in clear water
their wide-brimmed hats
will keep off
everything

on the boulevards meantime
carriages come and go
they carry
doctors to quiet basements
and children to circuses
music masters to doleful violins
and lovers to strange ceremonies
the fishermen are unimpressed

(by Alasdair Paterson) (adapted)

3.9 Rephrasing

Language Vocabulary / word order

Level Intermediate–Advanced

Age Any

This exercise allows students to develop their skills in the use of synonyms. The objective is to find different ways of expressing the same concept, while paying attention to small changes in meaning. This is a particularly useful skill for coping with the times when the person they are speaking to in a foreign language cannot understand them.

Procedure

1. Choose a sentence from a text which the class has seen recently, or which they are about to study, and dictate that sentence to the whole class. (An example of an alternative sentence is given below.) Individually, students try to rephrase the sentence so that it has the same meaning but using different words. To make this more difficult, don't allow any words from the original sentence to be used.
2. When everyone is ready, the sentences are read out.

> *One possible sentence:*
>
> 'To begin at the beginning:
> It is spring, moonless night in the small town, starless and bible-black, the cobblestreets silent . . .'
>
> (from Dylan Thomas: *Under Milk Wood*)

Variations

i) If you are working with an advanced class, this activity can also be used to practise the additional skill of recognising grammatical categories when dealing with difficult or unknown vocabulary. When students have got the idea of the exercise, ask them to rephrase a piece of 'nonsense' such as this:

> *Nonsense text for word-class recognition exercise:*
>
> 'Rumple had been snorking all day, and his broop was narfed.
> It was trittle for him to get to Respon by Venderfel, or his nasker would take over the lumpen.'

Don't allow the use of a dictionary, and explain that this isn't standard English.

ii) Instead of just rephrasing a passage to state the same meaning, students try to express the sense of the sentence in as few words as possible – an exercise in summarising which might be particularly useful for students of EAP or business English.

3.10 Writing!

Language All

Level Elementary upwards

Age Any

The usual method of setting a writing exercise is to give the students a title and a set amount of time in which to complete a story or other composition. This is then taken in and marked by the teacher. Typical titles for compositions might be 'A rainy day', 'The final journey', or 'Lost and found'.

It is easy to underestimate the possibilities of such traditional writing exercises. It can be great motivation for a student to produce a piece of work in a foreign language. Such exercises can go well beyond repetitive grammar revision, and the work of the students themselves can then be used as material for further language study, which is especially useful in an environment with few textual resources.

Variations

Furthermore, there are many ways of adding variety to writing exercises. Instead of the teacher marking the work, for example, half the lesson could be devoted to writing a composition, while in the other half of the lesson the texts could be swapped, read and marked either by individuals or by groups. To ease the potential for embarrassment, such exercises could be completed without having names written on the pieces of work.

The following points are also worth consideration:

i) Encouraging the use of imagination should help students to develop their capability for self expression in the target language. Think carefully about titles for stories – the simple ones are often the best, especially for young people.

ii) Try setting different types of written work: fiction, letters or speeches; advertisements or newspaper reports on sports and other events; instructions suitable for a recipe book or a 'how to' manual; even drama, poetry or limericks.

iii) If you have more than one class, why not arrange a 'pen-pal' letter exchange between students? You could encourage students to write to you about lessons, or other topics which they choose themselves.

iv) You could begin a 'problems page' pinned to the classroom wall, where students could anonymously submit problems, and others could pin up possible solutions.

There is almost limitless potential for variation, and the more directly relevant it is to students' needs and interests, the more successful it is likely to be.

4 Activities using blackboard, pens and paper

4.1 Dictogloss

Language Listening comprehension

Level Elementary upwards

Age Any

This is a well established dictation-based activity which helps to develop conscious listening skills in addition to an awareness of phrase and sentence structures.

Procedure

1. Choose a sentence suitable for the level of the class. This might be a sentence from a coursebook, but if so, make sure it is one which is not yet familiar to your students. An example sentence is given below. Tell the class that you will read this sentence to them once only. They should write down the key words as you read. You should not have to repeat the sentence, but with a large class you might like to read it once at the front of the room and once at the back. Students then work individually to try to recreate your sentence.
2. After a few minutes, elect a scribe. The class then works together to remember the whole sentence, which the scribe writes on the blackboard. When students have run out of ideas, read the original sentence one more time, and encourage them to get their version on the blackboard completely accurate. With the example overleaf, if you give the class the words 'Narcissus' and 'Oreads' on the board, these will act as anchors to help them with the order of the rest of the text.

Variation

Use a short paragraph or a whole short text, and ask students to get as close to the original as possible. Try to encourage correct grammar, but obviously the reproduction here is unlikely to be perfect!

> *Possible sentence for an upper-intermediate group:*
>
> When Narcissus died, the pool of his pleasure changed from a cup of sweet waters into a cup of salt tears, and the Oreads came weeping through the woodland that they might sing to the pool and give it comfort.
>
> (from Oscar Wilde's *The Disciple*)

Acknowledgement

This is another exercise which can be found in Davis and Rinvolucri's book *Dictation*, which is a very good investment for limited-resource teachers. (See also 'Dictation' (3.5) in this book.)

4.2 Ladders

Language Adjectives

Level Intermediate

Age Any

On many occasions, it is tempting to present lists of adjectives to students as if they are synonyms, whereas in reality the adjectives can vary greatly in degree. This activity raises awareness in learners, showing how adjectives often differ in strength.

Procedure

1. As a first example, write the following words on the blackboard:

   tiny, microscopic, small, little

2. Point out that these words do *not* mean exactly the same as each other. Then draw a 'ladder' on the blackboard, and ask students to suggest where on the ladder each word should go – smallest at the bottom, largest at the top. If possible, the whole class should agree on an order. There is probably no exactly correct answer, but as a general guide compare the order which the class decides on with this order:

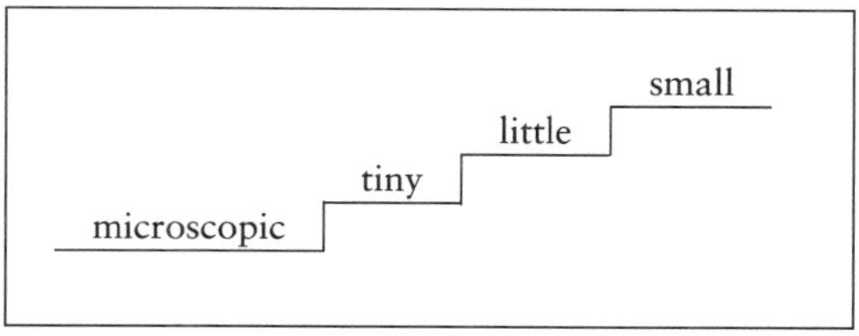

3. Now write these words on the blackboard:

   enormous, big, huge, gigantic, vast, large, king-size

4. Individually, each student now writes his or her own ladder to show the relationship between these adjectives. When they have done this, put students into pairs or small groups to decide a group order. Finally, try to produce a whole-class order. It might be something like this:

   big – large – king-size – huge – enormous – gigantic – vast

Examples

A thesaurus, if available, should provide other sets of adjectives which you can use, or you can try the following (in suggested ascending order):

> sluggish – slow – fast – quick – speedy – express
> dreadful – terrible – awful – bad – fine – good – great – wonderful – fantastic
> freezing – icy – cold – chilly – cool – tepid – warm – hot – boiling – scalding
> idiotic – stupid – silly – clever – smart – brainy – intelligent – wise – intellectual
> gloomy – dark – dim – dull – light – bright – vivid – dazzling

To highlight how some adjectives go better with some nouns than others, it can also be useful to ask students to write a short paragraph using each adjective with a different noun.

> *Example paragraph:*
>
> The man had bought a small camera, but there was a tiny problem. There was a microscopic scratch on the lens and little time to fix it before his holiday.

4.3 Picture to draw

Language Prepositions

Level Elementary upwards

Age Any

Procedure

1. Devise a simple line drawing, and a dictation to instruct students how to draw it. An example is given below.
2. Do this dictation in class without letting students see your drawing. Then appoint a scribe. The rest of the class tells the scribe how to recreate your drawing on the blackboard. This helps students to remember the words which you used in your dictation. When they are satisfied, show them your original picture.
3. Appoint a new scribe. The idea now is for the class to produce a picture of their own. Give each student a chance to 'dictate' a new element in the line drawing until it is complete. If you have a large class, you may need to produce two or three drawings so that everybody gets a chance to contribute.
4. Let students correct their own mistakes, which they will probably have to do for the scribe to understand them correctly; insist that they use English throughout the exercise.
5. The nature of the pictures will depend largely upon the character of the class rather than their language ability. It might therefore be a good follow up to use the drawings in the manner of doodles (see activity 2.5), and ask the class to suggest what the drawings might represent.

Example picture and dictation:

Draw a large circle in the centre of the page. Below this, draw a square which is about half the width of the circle and the same distance from the circle. Draw a line to connect the top, right corner of the square with the far right edge of the circle. Now do the same on the left side. In the top right corner of the page, there is a smaller circle. Three short lines are pointing away from the circle, but not touching it. What have you drawn?

5 Activities using other resources

5.1 Change chairs

Resources A chair for each student

Language 'If'

Level Elementary–Intermediate

Age Up to young adult

Procedure

1. Students sit on their chairs in a large circle. Ideally this is done in a large room or outside, but any reasonable, uncluttered space will do if there are no obvious physical restrictions to movement, and no dangerous pieces of furniture lying around.
2. The teacher stands in the middle of the circle – there is no chair for the teacher. He or she then gives the instruction:

   'Change chairs if you are wearing blue trousers.'

3. All students wearing blue trousers then have to stand up and find a new place in the circle, i.e. a place where another student with blue trousers was sitting. Meanwhile, the teacher sits in one of the vacated places.
4. This leaves a student in the centre of the circle. He or she must now do what the teacher has done – make a 'Change chairs if . . .' sentence, and then find a vacated chair to sit in. The objective is to get a chair back as soon as possible.

Rationale

This is a good energy raising exercise for those times when a class has reached its limit for concentration. If you work in a classroom with fixed furniture, taking the students outside and using coats as 'chairs' might give the exercise even more of a sense of fun. Carry on until everyone has had at least one or two turns in the centre – judge according to the size and enthusiasm of your group.

5.2 Going blind

Resources Furniture, one scarf, coins (or wrapped sweets)

Language Giving instructions

Level Elementary–Intermediate

Age Any

This is a particularly useful exercise for encouraging students to listen to each other in a foreign language. It is also good for confidence building.

Procedure

1. Ask for a volunteer. Blindfold the volunteer, who then sits in a corner of the room as you rearrange the furniture. (Even with fixed tables, you can do this by blocking the aisles with chairs or even other students.) The classroom is now something like a maze. Place a coin or wrapped sweet somewhere in the room.
2. Tell the blindfolded student what you have done, and explain that he or she will be directed to the coin by the other members of the class. The blindfolded student must find the coin without touching any furniture (remember – this includes other students).
3. Gently turn the student around two or three times to slightly confuse their sense of direction, then remain silent while the rest of the class gives instructions.
4. The blindfolded student has three 'lives'. A 'life' is lost each time a piece of furniture is touched, so after three touches the student is disqualified.
5. When a student finds the coin, he or she keeps it!
6. Other students will probably want to try this exercise, so have plenty of coins or sweets ready. Rearrange the furniture for each student.

Note

Safety is an important factor in this activity. Remain silent, but also stay close to the blindfolded student to prevent any accidents. Don't pile furniture up so that it might fall, and don't let other students touch the 'blind' one.

5.3 Hats

Resources Hats for the whole class; mirror (optional)

Language All

Level Intermediate–Advanced

Age Any

Preparation

Before the lesson, ask every student to bring an old hat from home. Students in most countries will be able to do this, but otherwise scarves, glasses or other 'accessories' would be suitable. It is advisable, however, to ask for old items which are no longer used by their owners, or the activity might become too personal. The exercise works best if students can be persuaded to swap hats in class, so that they can use one which they are not familiar with.

Procedure

1. Students put on the hats. If you have a mirror, they can look at themselves in the mirror. They should decide what sort of person might wear that sort of hat, and imagine details about that person:

   What do they like to eat?
   Whom do they like to spend time with?
   What do they do on Friday nights?
   etc.

2. If you have no mirror, have a 'fashion show' of hats, so that the whole class can decide the answers to these questions.
3. Then set up an everyday situation, such as going to the shop to buy some bananas, but finding that there aren't any available. Assign two 'hats' to two roles (such as shopkeeper and customer). Students act out how their 'hats' would react in this situation.

Note

In situations with greater resources, this can be done using masks. If you have this opportunity, be aware that the feelings generated by wearing masks are much greater than those generated by wearing hats. Make it clear that when you shout 'stop' at any point, students must immediately obey and remove their masks. Keith Johnstone's book *Impro* gives further guidance on the use of masks.

5.4 In the chair

Resources One chair

Language Question forms

Level Elementary upwards

Age Any

Procedure

1. The class thinks of a famous person (living or dead) whom they would like to interview. They then 'brainstorm' the questions which they would like to ask this person. This could be set for homework or done as a guided question-making exercise.
2. When you have a good supply of questions, ask for a volunteer to play the role of the famous person. The volunteer sits in a chair at the front of the class (or in the middle of a circle if you prefer), and is then asked the prepared questions by the other students, who play the part of radio or TV interviewers. Ensure that 'I' and 'you' are used throughout the interview.
3. From time to time you can swap the students around, so that several of them have the chance to 'be' the famous person.

Variations

i) A well-known variation on this theme is the 'balloon debate'. In this version, students role-play famous people who are travelling in a hot-air balloon which has started to drop towards the ocean. One of the occupants of the balloon will have to jump out so that the lives of the others can be saved.

Each famous person is given two minutes to try to explain why they are so important to the world that they cannot possibly be thrown out of the balloon. After the arguments of the famous people have all been heard, a class vote is taken to decide which of them should jump out of the balloon.

This 'debate' can be more successful if students pick the names of their 'characters' at random from a list of people which you have prepared. This can stimulate the imagination, and doesn't impose any ethical decision-making on their choice of famous people.

ii) Alternatively in the 'balloon debate' scenario, instead of using named individuals, each student can represent a profession, arguing why their category (journalist, nurse, politician, teacher, etc.) is more essential than the others.

5.5 Picture postcards

Resources Pens, paper and postcards

Language Descriptions

Level Intermediate–Advanced

Age Any

Procedure

1. Give each student a picture postcard. These might be available for sale locally, or you might like to build up a collection whenever you can.
2. Each student must look at his or her picture, and imagine what it is like to be in that place. On a separate sheet of paper he or she then writes a brief message to a friend, just as with a real postcard, describing the place and what has been happening there.
3. Take the postcards and the messages back, and separate them. Give each postcard a number and each message a letter, but don't list the matching messages and cards in the same order. Distribute the cards around the classroom, placing each one with a message from a different card.
4. Students then walk around the classroom, looking at all the messages and postcards. They must decide which message goes with which postcard, and write this down, e.g. message B with postcard 5. At the end, check the answers. You might like to ask how certain answers were decided.

Note

If your postcards have place names on them, you will have to forbid the use of these names in the messages. The numbers on the backs of the postcards and messages provide a point of reference for answers and discussion.

5.6 Read all about it!

Resources Pens, paper, newspaper articles

Language All

Level Intermediate–Advanced

Age Young adult upwards

Preparation

Take an English language newspaper, or a collection of articles which you might have built up over a period of time. Choose one article for about every four students in your class, and write two comprehension questions for each article. The level of difficulty can be adjusted according to the students.

Procedure

Mix the comprehension questions up, and dictate them to the class. Then place the newspaper articles around the classroom. Explain that each article contains the answers to two questions. Students work individually; they move around the classroom trying to find the answers to your questions.

Variation

For less advanced classes, it is a useful exercise for students to write their own comprehension questions.

Give each group of four students an article, and tell them to prepare ten questions based on the content of that article.

Students are then set a time limit in which to answer as many of the other groups' questions as possible. The timing will depend on the size of the class, although as a general guideline 10–15 minutes per ten questions is reasonable – but don't expect everyone to answer all the questions.

If the class enjoys discussion, groups could prepare an eleventh question on the model of 'Do you think . . . ?'. Then, when all the answers have been checked, they can continue with a group discussion based on the issues raised.

5.7 Talk

Resources Teacher's watch

Language All

Level Advanced

Age Any

This is a game in which the winner is the person speaking when the one minute 'bell' sounds (or when the teacher shouts 'Time's up!').

Procedure

1. A subject or title is given to the class, and one student is asked to start. This student must talk about the subject without hesitation, repetition or inaccuracy (in either content or language). If another student spots one of these, he or she may challenge the speaker by calling 'Challenge!', at which point the clock 'stops'.
2. The teacher can act as chief judge, but should consult the rest of the class in deciding if a challenge is correct or not. If a challenge is judged to be good, then the challenger must attempt to talk about the subject for the remaining portion of the 60 seconds.

Possible topics:

Cooking; countries (France, Germany, etc.); famous people, films or TV programmes; hobbies (fishing, photography, etc.); holidays; local festivals or celebrations; pets; recently studied texts; school subjects.

Variation

If a challenge is accepted, instead of continuing with the same topic, the challenger is given a new topic to talk about, but only for the remaining time period.

Acknowledgement

This is adapted from the BBC Radio 4 game 'Just a minute' in the programme 'I'm sorry I haven't a clue'.

5.8 Tourists

Resources Picture postcards

Language Simple questions

Level Intermediate

Age Any

Preparation

Prepare a set of picture postcards (or pictures cut from a glossy magazine). This exercise works best if the pictures are of places known to the class.

Procedure

1. In turn, each student takes one postcard, and imagines that he or she is in that place. He or she then mimes doing something which is typical for that place. For example, a student with a postcard of Piccadilly Circus might mime trying to cross the road; a postcard of Buckingham Palace might inspire a mime of watching the Queen – or even being the Queen.
2. As the mime continues, the other students ask yes/no questions to find out more details about where this place is:

   'Can you see many trees?'
   'Is it very hot?'
   'Are you somebody famous?'
   etc.

3. When the place has been successfully guessed, you might wish to follow this up with a 'brainstorming' session to find out what else students know about it. This would fit in nicely with the students' natural wish to see the postcard which they have been talking about.

Variation

If your resources do not stretch to a collection of postcards, this can also be done more simply by using pieces of paper with place names written on them. In this case, because there are no visual clues to help students, you should be certain that all the place names are familiar to the class.

5.9 Who am I?

Resources Sticky labels, pens

Language Simple questions

Level Elementary upwards

Age Young adult upwards

Procedure

1. Organise the class into a sequence of either a line, rows, or a circle.
2. Each student is given a pen and a sticky label. On the label they write the name of a famous person. It can be anyone, of any nationality, living or dead. They then stick this label onto the forehead of the person before them in the sequence. (The first person sticks it on the forehead of the last person.) Students should not know what is written on their own foreheads.
3. The objective is for each student to ask the person who gave them their label yes/no questions to discover what the name on their own forehead is. Questions such as:

   'Am I still alive?'
   'Am I a woman?'

   If the answer to a question is 'yes', the questioner can continue to another question. If the answer is 'no', the next person in the sequence has a turn at asking questions.
4. The exercise can go on for as long as the sticky labels last. A new name is allocated each time one is guessed correctly.

Variation

Instead of following a fixed sequence of 'questioner–answerer', students get up and walk around the room. They can ask anyone they meet yes/no questions as above. If you have no sticky labels, almost the same effect can be achieved by using pieces of card tucked in at the back of students' trouser/skirt waistlines.

References

Ali, O. 1996 'The Lonely Man' (trans. Nandy, P.). Internet: WWW-site http://cmgm.stanford.edu/~ahmad/omarali.html #omarali2

Boal, A. 1992 *Games for Actors and Non-Actors.* London: Routledge.

Davis, P. and Rinvolucri, M. 1988 *Dictation.* Cambridge: Cambridge University Press.

Irving, J. 1993 *Trying To Save Piggy Sneed.* London: Black Swan.

Johnstone, K. 1981 *Impro.* London: Methuen.

McGough, R. (ed.) 1982 *Strictly Private.* Harmondsworth: Puffin.

Rinvolucri, M. 1984 *Grammar Games.* Cambridge: Cambridge University Press.

Sacks, O. 1986 *The Man Who Mistook His Wife For A Hat.* London: Picador.

Stoppard, T. 1968 *Rosencrantz And Guildenstern Are Dead.* London: Faber.

Thomas, D. 1985 *Under Milk Wood.* London: Everyman.

Trilling, L. and Bloom, H. (eds.) 1973 *Victorian Prose and Poetry.* Oxford: Oxford University Press.

Ur, P. 1981 *Discussions That Work.* Cambridge: Cambridge University Press.

Bibliography for limited-resource situations

An asterisk (*) indicates a book particularly highly recommended for teachers working with limited time and resources.

ELT classroom activities

*Davis, P. and Rinvolucri, M. 1988 *Dictation*. Cambridge: Cambridge University Press.

An extremely useful volume of varied activities using dictation. Some photocopying is needed for some activities, and one section relies on the availability of telephones, but most exercises can be adapted to any circumstances.

Frank, C., Rinvolucri, M. and Berer, M. 1982 *Challenge To Think*. Oxford: Oxford University Press.

A good collection of puzzles and questionnaires which can be presented to students orally. But sections with photographs and large amounts of texts for presentation are less flexible without multiple class copies.

Klippel, F. 1984. *Keep Talking*. Cambridge: Cambridge University Press.

Although several of the activities are designed for photocopying, the aims of the exercises are clearly set out, and can be adapted for use in a limited-resource environment.

Lee, W. 1979. *Language Teaching Games and Contests*. Oxford: Oxford University Press.

A large collection of games, often using few or no facilities. The focus, however, is primarily on younger learners, and there is little for teenagers or adults.

*Lindstromberg, S. (ed.) 1990. *The Recipe Book*. Harlow: Pilgrims Longman.

Contains many zero-facility exercises from different sources, although some activities require special resources (dice, playing cards, dictionaries). The approach is humanistic, and teachers will find several things they can use in any situation.

Morgan, J. and Rinvolucri, M. 1988. *The Q Book*. Harlow: Longman.

Many activities require a great deal of photocopying for immediate and practical use, but their basic ideas can be adapted for use in a limited-resource environment.

Rinvolucri, M. 1984. *Grammar Games*. Cambridge: Cambridge University Press.

Several games involving work with sentences and short texts (see '2.14 Sentence Games') make this a useful book. Some of the more complex games require photocopying or a large amount of preparation before they can be used. The 1995 'sister' book *More Grammar Games* (Rinvolucri and Davis) requires similar access to resources.

*Ur, P. 1981. *Discussions That Work*. Cambridge: Cambridge University Press.

A compact and comprehensive survey of discussion activities. A handful of activities require pictures or photographs; others require role cards. Many of the activities, however, are suitable for transfer to any teaching situation.

*Ur, P. and Wright, A. 1992. *Five-Minute Activities*. Cambridge: Cambridge University Press.

Many short activities and fillers, easy to set up, but frequently requiring a blackboard. Contains useful sets of example language to use in activities.

Drama activities

*Boal, A. 1992. *Games for Actors and Non-Actors*. London: Routledge.

Contains over 150 pages of drama activities, many of which can be adapted for an ELT focus. Also contains valuable examples of how these activities have worked in the past.

Johnstone, K. 1981. *Impro*. London: Methuen.

Sets up many ideas for encouraging creativity with language and movement in a drama workshop situation. One section relies on the availability of masks. Many of the activities are 'hidden' in the text.

Maley, A. and Duff, A. 1982 (2nd ed.). *Drama Techniques in Language Learning*. Cambridge: Cambridge University Press.

A wide selection of drama activities, usually with a language focus. Some materials are required.

Reference material

Byrne, D. 1986 (2nd ed.). *Teaching Oral English*. Harlow: Longman.

A good pedagogical reference book. Many of the examples given, however, rely on pictures or objects for stimuli.

*Swan, M. 1980. *Practical English Usage*. Oxford: Oxford University Press.

A clear and comprehensive summary of many awkward points of English grammar. An excellent reference for teachers. The later edition is less portable than its forerunner.

Wright, A, 1993 (2nd ed.). *1000+ Pictures for Teachers to Copy*. London: Nelson.

Clear instructions and examples for drawing on the blackboard, if that is your preferred method of presenting material.

Textual material

Christie, A. 1993. *Poirot's Early Cases*. London: HarperCollins.

A good selection of short stories as a source for puzzles and short texts.

Conan-Doyle, A. 1992 (facsimile ed.). *The Adventures of Sherlock Holmes*. Ware: Wordsworth Classics.

A convenient (and cheap!) edition containing 24 short stories featuring the famous detective as well as two longer adventures. Very useful for ideas for puzzle activities (see 1.21 'Puzzle story'). It also contains material suitable for use as short texts in other activities described in this book.

Heaney, S. and Hughes, T. (eds.). 1982. *The Rattle Bag*. London: Faber.

A large and varied collection of poetry, containing something which should be of interest to most students (see 3.7 'Poems alive' and 3.8 'Poetry points'). The book, although thick, is not too unwieldy for travelling with or using in the classroom.

Irving, J. 1983. *Trying To Save Piggy Sneed*. London: Black Swan.

An accessible collection of (American) short stories, many of which contain passages which can be adapted for classroom use.

Jones, E. (ed.). 1987. *British Short Stories of Today*. Harmondsworth: Penguin.

Several good short stories including cultural notes to the texts. An edition of American stories is also available.

*Maley, A. 1993, 1995 *Short and Sweet* (Volumes 1 and 2). Harmondsworth: Penguin.

Excellent collections of short texts suitable for dictating or presenting on the blackboard. Accompanying activities make these two volumes a valuable resource.

Index according to language activity type